Shelley-
I'm so glad God put
you & John in our lives.

KEEP
WALKING

I'm very sorry about what
you've faced over the past months
but you've been a Champion.

By STEVEN GREEN

You aren't in this alone, Paris,
I & more importantly, God is
in this with you! Keep walking
because God has great things ahead
for you —

Purpose Books

DEDICATION

To my wife, Pamala: Thank you for loving me over the last 42 years. Since October 18,1982, you have been an encourager, nurse, advocate, and prayer warrior on my behalf during some very dark days. I can't imagine this journey without you by my side. Throughout this time, you have slept in chairs, on hospital cots and sofas, even in the car parked in hospital garages so that you could be close to me and make sure I received the care I needed.

To my sons, Brandon and Christopher: Thank you for your unwavering love and support. You have never complained about being taken down a path that was not of your choosing. You have always been there for me. I will always love you.

To Jan Madden: Thank you for pushing me to write this book. When I thought I couldn't do it, you encouraged me to keep writing.

To Karen Hatcher: Thank you for your untiring and selfless efforts in helping a non-writer put on the page what I felt in my heart.

TABLE OF CONTENTS

Chapter 1

SEVERE!

"This is a 21-year-old male," someone with me said. "No previously known medical issues. He fell from a five-story building..."

"No," the doctor interrupted. "There is no way he fell from a five-story building and is still alive."

"I saw where he fell from. He fell five stories."

One of the top neurosurgeons in the United States stood beside my bed at Methodist Hospital in Houston Medical Center as hospital staff prepared for my 86th major surgery. My wife and I deem surgeries major only if I spend a night in the hospital post-surgery. I lost track of day procedures years ago and have no idea how many days, weeks, and months at a time I have spent in the hospital.

We arrived on November 30, 2021, at 6:00 am. As soon as I was prepped for surgery, the neurosurgeon took me by the arm and said, "I'll walk back with you to the operating room." I kissed my wife good-bye one final time and watched her depart through double swinging doors as they began pushing me down the long corridor to surgery. The neurosurgeon explained the laminectomy was a common surgery he had performed thousands of times over 40-plus years and would perform another that same week. As we reached the operating room and they pushed me through the swinging double doors, his final words to me were, "You should be awake and ready to leave the hospital by noon, but I'll leave that decision up to you. If you feel like going home or staying overnight, it's up to you. Let me know what you wish, and I'll make it happen".

I had experienced severe pain in the back of both legs down to the back of my knees. I wrestled back pain for many years, but the leg pain was new and erupted only a few months prior to surgery. It first started with painful muscle cramps in both legs during the night and lasted longer than any other leg cramps I experienced. Walking eventually became a painful chore that worsened over a short period of time. When I walked very far, it felt as if I had concrete boots on my feet. The pain from walking and the nightly cramps reached an unbearable point. I finally decided I could bear no more so I made an appointment with an orthopedic surgeon, Dr. Moore. He immediately ordered an MRI of my back.

We returned weeks later to Dr. Moore's office for a follow-up visit. Dr. Moore handed my wife, Pamala, a copy of the radiologist's report and wanted us to follow along. As he read the report, he paused three different times when the word "severe" was used to describe injuries in three different parts of my back. Dr. Moore looked up from the report and told us I had a serious problem that needed immediate attention. Instead of his usual jovial personality, he was serious and to the point. He showed images of the areas discussed in the report and told us the lumbar area was the worst of the three. He told me the L3, L4, L5 and S1 needed immediate surgical intervention. The MRI showed the spinal cord flattened over a large area due to arthritis. My spinal cord was so compressed that there was little, if any, spinal fluid getting through that area.

Dr. Moore turned around on his stool and looked at my wife and I straight in the eye and in a serious manner he told us Dr. Robert Parrish was the only surgeon he trusted to perform the surgery. Dr. Parrish worked at Houston Methodist Hospital in the Houston Medical Center and was considered one of the top three neurosurgeons in the United States. Dr. Parrish had been a neurosurgeon for 40 years, was in his early 70s, and had a long, distinguished career in dealing with severe neurological cases. Although the laminectomy was a common procedure, Dr. Moore said the condition of my spinal cord dictated someone with Dr. Parrish's experience.

I asked Dr. Moore if there were any other options besides surgery. Visiting a pain management specialist over the previous two years produced little, if any, improvement. I wasn't looking forward to another surgery. Dr. Moore said I could either let Dr. Parrish perform the laminectomy and spinal fusion or discuss a comfortable wheelchair in which I would spend the rest of my life. We felt there was no option but to go to Houston.

We arrived at Methodist Hospital and sat down with Dr. Parrish. I asked Dr. Parrish if there were any other options besides surgery. His answer was the same Dr. Moore had given. He said surgery would give me the freedom to do some things that I hadn't done in quite a while, but it would take a month or so post-surgery to get there. Without surgery, my nerves would be permanently damaged in the next 60 days, would not be regenerated, and I would spend the rest of my life in a wheelchair. Dr. Parrish said everything from the waist down would be paralyzed and there would be little, if any, hope of reversing the paralysis. I couldn't imagine being paralyzed and in a wheelchair for the rest of my life. I looked at my wife and we both quickly agreed we would move forward with the procedure. The surgery was set for Nov. 30, 2021, the Tuesday after Thanksgiving and just three weeks away. During those three weeks, the pain and heaviness in my legs grew worse each day. I was more than ready to have the surgery and for the pain and heaviness in my legs to be gone.

On the day of surgery, Dr. Parrish walked me back to the operating room and went to prepare for the surgery. I was placed on the operating room table and quickly readied for anesthesia. I always hate those few moments before being put to sleep for surgery. My ears ring and I'm anxious about the level of pain I will experience after the procedure. The surgery was to be no more than two hours long.

I instantly knew when I woke up that I was in the recovery room, and I was in the greatest amount of pain I have ever experienced in all the previous 85 surgeries. My legs hurt in the same place they had hurt prior to surgery, but now the pain was excruciating. I screamed uncontrollably at the top of my lungs. I was quickly given medication to put me back to sleep. When I awoke, I was in an elevator and being transported to my hospital room. When I saw people in the elevator, I tried to control the verbal expression of pain, but the pain was too great. I was given another round of medication. The next time I awoke, I was in the hospital room, screaming in agony. It was far greater than any pain I had ever experienced. Pain medication had little effect. The surgeon was called, and the room filled with nursing staff and doctors who administered more powerful medication. Again, it had little to no effect. My wife later told me she was called to my room and could immediately hear my screams when she stepped off the elevator. Doctors gave me an IV medication that put me back to sleep. This time when I awoke, I was still in great pain, though it had somewhat lessened. As I turned my head, I could see it was dark outside and knew it was much later than 12 noon. At that moment, I heard a nurse talking to my wife.

"Has your husband been awake long enough for you to tell him everything that has gone wrong, and all the serious issues Dr. Parrish discovered during the surgery?"

Little did I know, the next several months to follow, our deep faith in God would be tested like never before.

Chapter 2

PAIN AND SORROWS

I have experienced pain every day since 10:10 a.m., October 18, 1982. Some days it has been unbearable and tolerable on other days, but not one day has gone by since my accident that I have not been in some level of pain.

I was working in construction on a condominium complex in the University of Texas area. I had taken my normal 10 a.m. break, gulping down my usual Dr. Pepper and Snickers candy bar, before I climbed the stairs to the fourth floor. I then climbed another floor to the top of a scaffold on which I had been working for over a week. The scaffold collapsed in what seemed like slow motion, and I fell backwards to the ground. I grazed tiny limbs of a small tree just an instant before hitting the ground which righted me on my feet. It was as if a bomb exploded inside my body as I crashed into the ground. My first thought was, "I'M ALIVE!" I never lost consciousness and was amazed that not even the breath was knocked out of me. It did seem as if everything around me had gone totally silent and nothing near me was moving. I sat up and immediately saw body parts that were bent in abnormal directions. Slowly, the noise came back as people quickly rushed to where I had fallen. I assume, due to shock, that I still wasn't in a great deal of pain until they lifted me to take me just a few blocks to Brackenridge Hospital, the trauma hospital for Austin and surrounding counties.

I was rushed into the emergency room and heard a doctor ask for more details.

"This is a 21-year-old male," someone with me said. "No previously known medical issues. He fell from a five-story building..."

"No," the doctor interrupted. "There is no way he fell from a five-story building and is still alive."

"I saw where he fell from. He fell five stories."

It would be a long day of tests and x-rays. At that time, the hospital didn't have an MRI machine. Many doctors from various fields kept coming and going. I was given a lot of medications in my IV as my pain level increased. A nurse came to my bedside shortly after we arrived and asked if I had family, I wanted her to contact. I explained that my wife was expecting our first child in five months, and I wanted my father to be the one to tell her what had taken place. My father was the pastor of a church in south Austin and Pamala was the church receptionist. I explained it wouldn't be unusual for someone to call the church and ask to speak to Pastor Green. The nurse could tell my father, Homer Green, what had taken place. I hoped the baby wouldn't be affected when he told my wife.

Thankfully, my dad was able to break the news to my wife and take her to the hospital. Word spread quickly. The hospital waiting area was filled with people from our church. I was able to see my wife after what seemed an eternity of blood draws, x-rays, and other tests. It was a memorable reunion with lots of tears and hugs. This moment marked the start of a journey in which my wife and I would spend the next 40 years in and out of doctor's offices, hospitals, and rehabilitation facilities. Her embrace is always what I look forward to the most. Even with all the noise that takes place on most hospital floors, I can almost always pick out my wife's footsteps in the hospital hallway. No pain medication does for me what her arriving at my bedside does to ease my mind and pain.

About 7 p.m., a doctor came to the ER and said more testing needed to be performed, but the x-rays had shown broken bones; many crushed and turned into powder. The bones would not be easily repaired. Miraculously, there were no internal or head injuries that needed immediate attention. He said the best plan of action would be to wait until the next morning to surgically explore various areas and make some of the most urgent repairs. That would be the first of over 90 surgeries requiring us to spend at least one night in the hospital.

At 11 p.m., my room finally fell silent after all my family, friends, and doctors left my room. My wife stayed. The bed began to shake in the quietness as I began to realize how close to death I had come. Up to that point, I was kept occupied with hospital staff, testing, and family. I began to dwell on what had taken place.

At 6AM the next day, I was taken back for my first surgery on my right leg, right ankle, and foot. They were the most badly damaged. The surgeons took out 40 percent of my right ankle due to the large amount of crushed bone. Using rods, pins, screws, and plates, they did the best they could to put my leg, ankle, and foot back together and placed my leg in a cast from the knee to my foot.

When I returned from surgery to my room, I dozed off and immediately had a nightmare taking me back to the accident site. In my dream, I stood on the scaffolding at the condominium, watching myself fall backwards. Just before I hit the ground in my dream, I jerked so hard in real life that I pulled some of the repaired areas of bone out of place. My wife called the nursing staff who then called the doctors. X-rays revealed that I had pulled my ankle out of place. This same nightmare occurred almost every time I fell asleep.

I thought I would be good as new after a few surgeries. I asked the doctor after several procedures how long it would be before I started running again. His response should have given me a clue of what the future held for us.

"We aren't even sure if you'll ever walk again," the doctor said. "If you can ever learn to walk, then we will talk about running." I still wasn't thinking that I would deal with this for the rest of my life.

After several weeks of numerous surgeries, a physical therapist attempted to make me stand. I thought I would show them. I will stand up and show them that I'm not as bad as they keep saying I am, even though I was in pain from head to toe. I sat up in the bed a couple of times since arriving at the hospital. I thought standing wouldn't be that difficult. The therapist went through her list of things to do and not do. She put the gait belt around my waist and gave the command to slowly stand. Before I got all the way to my feet, I almost fainted from the pain. I immediately fell back into bed. I was nauseated and was soon throwing up. The pain was overwhelming and far more than I expected. The therapist changed plans the next day and decided to have me work on just sitting on the side of the bed.

I grew up during a time where I constantly heard, "don't whine," "don't complain," and "tough it out." I remember when I was 16, I got hit in the mouth with a baseball and my mom took me to the local hospital emergency room. The doctor took about an hour to arrive. When I was taken back to one of the rooms where he sewed me up, I remarked that he had taken a long time to get there. He said, "I'm always having my dinner interrupted by one of you boys to sew something up. I thought I would take my time to eat one dinner with my family without being interrupted."

I never wanted to show pain or show that someone had hurt me. My brother, Richard, tells the story of when we were in high school playing a football game against a team that played dirty from start to finish. It wasn't enough to tackle you. They tackled you, then gave you an elbow in the stomach or a poke in the eye. After Richard was tackled on one play, he stayed down on the ground in pain. I picked him up by the back of his shoulder pads, scooped him to his feet and partly carried him back to the huddle. As we made our way to the huddle, I told him he couldn't let the other team know they had hurt him. I didn't care if his leg was broken, I didn't want him to show one sign of pain until we got to the huddle where we could check it out.

That was how I lived up until October 18, 1982. Don't complain, don't show pain, don't let the other guy know he hurt you. Do whatever it takes to keep from showing pain.

Now, I struggled to get to my feet. I couldn't help but show pain. I tried my best to hide it, but I just couldn't. I struggled for days just to sit on the side of the bed without getting nauseated. It took days to reach a point where I could stand, but I got nauseated each time I stood. Eventually, I made it to the hospital door before collapsing in the wheelchair and vomiting. I was embarrassed, because I had never been able to not "bounce back" or "just push through" the pain. This pain was far beyond anything I had ever experienced.

Doctors were planning the next round of surgeries when they told us that this would be our life for some years to come. They scheduled the next surgery as soon as we finished the previous surgery. I needed to be put back together. The bones that had turned to powder could not be put back together. Since the planned surgeries were not emergency in nature, the surgeons thought it would benefit me to get out of the hospital for a few weeks and take some time to clear my head. Life had drastically changed in a moment's time, and it had been one surgery after another. Pamala and I needed time to regroup before moving forward.

It was wonderful to get home, though I was in pain constantly and could do very little besides go from the sofa to the bed. I pleaded with my wife to take me back to the condominiums so I could see the accident site. I'm not sure why, but I was drawn back to that area. I wanted to see where I fell. The condos had a parking garage for the first floor, so we were able to pull up near the place I landed. With great effort and my wife's help, I got out of the car and got to the place where I had landed.

"Hey, aren't you the guy who fell?" an electrician on the job site asked. "When you fell, I went straight to my car and left the job site. I didn't want to be here when they came to get your body."

This marked the first of many times my wife and I would return to that particular site and give thanks to God for sparing my life.

Chapter 3

MY BEGINNINGS

I have lived a blessed life. My parents, Homer, and Sheryl Green, both grew up in the small, east Texas town of Kilgore (population 10,000). My father worked as a machinist and my mother was a stay-at- home mom. They were both very much involved in the church which was attended by well over 200 people each Sunday morning. My dad was asked to preach a special youth event, though he had never preached before. He felt God dealing with him about going into ministry and this invitation propelled him to follow God's leading. He would soon preach revivals and youth rallies in many of the northeast Texas churches. After a year of preaching in the area, he felt God calling him even deeper into ministry. In the fall of 1969, my parents made the difficult decision to move to Houston so my father could attend Texas Bible College.

I was six years old, and my brother Richard was three when we moved to an area northeast of downtown Houston to be near Stonewall Pentecostal Church. The pastor, O.W. Williams, had been my parents' childhood pastor in Kilgore and performed their wedding when they were in their early 20s. Stonewall was a large, thriving church and the people were fond of the pastor.

My father drove about 45 minutes each morning to Texas Bible College. He would then drive to Baker

Hughes Machine, one of the larger Houston area machine shops, where he would work the second shift and then drive home. My dad was gone in the mornings when my brother and I woke up and would get home after we went to bed. Every night before putting us to bed, my mom gathered us near her and would pray for about an hour. In the first five to 10 minutes, she asked Richard and I to pray for our dad, grandparents, and other family. Then, she would pray for the next 45 to 50 minutes as we sat nearby. Those are fond memories that helped establish the importance of prayer much later in my life as I faced some difficult and dark days.

My father took a position at Prudential Insurance while attending Texas Bible College. When I was seven, my sister Angela was born. When I was eight, my father became pastor of a church in Liberty, Texas, a small town on the east side of Houston, while still attending Texas Bible College. He enjoyed working for Prudential Insurance and the income was greater than working as a machinist. His work as pastor, insurance salesman, and college attendee took a lot of his time, but he was successful at all three.

The small church often needed money to meet the monthly bills, so my mom made peanut brittle in our home kitchen and took the three of us kids downtown to sell to local businesses. The money we made helped pay both the church and personal bills. As a child, I never felt the struggles I now know that my parents experienced.

My dad decided to leave Prudential Insurance to pastor full time. One of the top managers for the Houston area tried convincing my dad to rethink his decision. The manager told my dad that if he stayed, he would no longer need to worry about money. He was a rising star in the company.

Leaving a great income to be a full-time pastor took commitment and much prayer. When I was 11, we moved back to Kilgore. My dad was somewhat anxious about becoming the pastor of his childhood church, but the church accepted him as its pastor, and we would see the blessing of God. This church was great for me, a young boy about to enter my teens. There were a lot of boys within a three-year range of my age. Both sets of grandparents were a bicycle ride away and we always had a lot of activity around our home. Other family members attended the church and lived nearby. I quickly made many friends, some of whom I am still friends with 50 years later.

It seemed evangelists and missionaries always stayed in our home. It wasn't unusual for our backyard to be filled with kids playing some sport such as baseball or football. The evangelists or missionaries who stayed with us often joined us in whatever game we played. With the help of my grandfather, we put up a basketball goal on the edge of the church parking lot and outlined a volleyball court. Our lives were built around the church and doing church activities.

When I turned 15, my dad bought me a car. I didn't have a driver's license, but I was allowed to go where I wanted. Sunday nights were the most enjoyable times each week. After church, our youth met other area church youth for pizza in Longview, a town of about 50,000. Our favorite pizza restaurant was Mr. Gatti's Pizza. By 9 p.m., the restaurant was full of young people coming from their Sunday night services.

I never expected Mr. Gatti's would be the place I would meet the girl who would become my wife. She walked in with her best friend, whom I had known for several years. They walked over to the table where I sat with my best friend, and we chatted for a few minutes. Since I was attracted to this new girl, I asked if they would join us at our table. She introduced herself as Pamala Soules and told me she had lived in Longview before moving to Abilene. After that night, we wrote letters and talked on the phone almost daily. I was 19 and in college. She was 16 and the most beautiful girl I had ever met. I wasn't thinking about marriage, but for the first time, I found myself drawn to a girl. We married a few years later.

After 41 years of marriage, I can say that I'm so glad God placed her in my life that night. God knew what was to come and knew I needed someone strong and able to handle the great challenges that would put a strain on any marriage, causing many to fall apart.

Not long after the night I met Pamala, I felt the call to ministry. In the fall of 1980, I left Kilgore Community College to attend Texas Bible College in Houston. I had no doubt God called me into ministry. I grew up with the church as the focal point of everything I did. I received the Holy Ghost as a young boy, but I was not totally committed to God. I loved church, I loved THE church. I enjoyed being around the church and working with those who attended church. I didn't care for most of what the world held, but church was where I had fun, spent time with friends, and even had great experiences with God. However, I had not yet developed my own personal walk with God outside the church.

The summer after my first year of Bible college, my wife and I married. We attended another year of college before leaving Houston and moving to Austin where my father now pastored a large, thriving and rapidly growing church. Once again, our life was built around the church. Almost every night, there was some event at the church.

My wife and I preached in the Austin area. When ministers were on vacation or out of town, my wife and I filled in for those pastors. Even though my life was consumed with church work, I felt God wanted me to make a greater commitment to Him. I had experienced several miracles in my life, but I had not developed the daily disciplines needed to fully capture all that God could do through me.

My accident forced me to slow down a little. I was forced to trust in God and not my own abilities or understanding. My wife and I found ourselves leaning on God's timing as we faced challenges in every area of our lives. We had car payments, house payments, and normal bills like other young growing families, but I was no longer able to work. After the accident, our lives rotated around hospitals and doctor bills. We were consumed with x-rays, blood work, surgical procedures, and physical therapy appointments. We learned what it really meant to trust in God. He was our only hope for my health, and our only hope for financial security and raising our family. We learned how to pray and allow God to lead us.

Chapter 4

MORE TRAUMA

Additional surgeries were scheduled, but I was glad to be released from the hospital for a few weeks for the holidays. We decided to make the five-hour trip to family in northeast Texas. My mom went with us. I made the trip by lying down in the back seat. It was great to be back at my grandparents' house where I spent so much time growing up. It felt great to take our minds off everything we had been through over the past few weeks. It felt great to snuggle in the bed in which I spent so many nights as a young boy. However, my wife awoke in great pain during the night. I called my mom who was five minutes away at her parents' house. She quickly dressed, picked us up, and took us to the local emergency room. The medical staff assumed I was the patient because of all the casts and other medical dressings I sported. We let them know my wife was in the car, experiencing what we thought were possible labor pains and she wasn't due for another four months. They quickly took her back and examined her for some time. The doctor started making plans to take the baby for the health of my wife. She said there was little chance the baby would survive.

After a few quick questions, I asked the doctor if I could see my wife. Pamala was in less pain due to the medication, but the fear of losing her first baby could be seen in her face. My mom and I prayed in the waiting area and called family to pray. The doctor said the only option was to take the baby. After more prayer, I asked the doctor about the possibility of driving back to Austin where our doctors could perform the procedure if they deemed it necessary. The doctor advised against it, but we wanted to be sure there were no other options before we let her take our child. Finally, the doctor relented. We got in the car and my mom drove us the long five hours back to Austin. We prayed during the entire trip. My mom drove probably faster than she had ever driven. The sun was just rising on the horizon as we entered the outskirts of Austin. The doctor was waiting on us He did a thorough examination and saw no evidence of what the east Texas doctor reported. He said there was certainly no reason the baby couldn't go full term. He gave my wife medication to help her sleep.

Miraculously, our first child was born healthy and without any issues in March 1983.

Chapter 5

THE NEW 'NORMAL'

Though God performed the miraculous to spare our son's life, it seemed we faced challenges on all sides. The life I lived up to October 18, 1982, had been turned upside down. We struggled with financial and health challenges. We realized the need for those daily spiritual disciplines that keep GOD close with you in those times. My wife and I had boxes of bills and it seemed as if we lived in the doctor's office or hospital. As soon as one surgery was performed, another issue would arise. It was at this time my wife and I learned the importance of personal daily devotion. That meant daily prayer and daily time in God's Word. It was no longer about just attending church services and events but allowing God to speak to us. If I could pick one thing that helped us get through all that we have faced, it is our turn toward God at this time. We learned that OUR prayers could touch Heaven and change the doctor's report from bad to good. Our prayers could help us overcome the financial struggles we faced. We realized God would hear our prayers and show His miracle-working power.

God had performed miracles in my life from my birth. When I was born, the doctor walked out of the operating room and told my parents' pastor, "I've done all I can do. If this woman lives, it is because of what you do, Pastor." The doctor said the delivery was so difficult for him that he would not deliver another baby. He practiced medicine for many more years, but I was the last baby he delivered. Not only did my mother survive, but she would also go on to have two more children.

When I was eight and my brother five, we had our tonsils removed at Houston Methodist, the same hospital I had my back surgery. The medical staff took my brother back before taking me back. Minutes later, doctors told my parents they feared my brother and I wouldn't survive because they couldn't control our bleeding. My parents called their pastor at the time, Bro. O. W. Williams. We walked out of the hospital a few days later.

God had already done so much in my life. Now, He miraculously spared my life from a five-story fall! Not only did he spare my life, but he spared me from paralysis and head trauma. We became sold out to God and gave everything to Him. We began to see God's hand at work in our personal lives but would still face many more trials and times of great struggle.

In the spring of 1983, our first son, Brandon, was born. I reached a point where I could start daily outpatient physical therapy. I still had the mindset that somehow this wasn't going to be a lifetime experience. I thought if I could get to physical therapy, it would be like going to the gym. I would get back in shape and be my old self. Before my accident, I lifted weights and ran daily. I ran downtown and back each night. Once downtown, I enjoyed running by the lighted store fronts in the peace and quiet of a small town. For years, I relaxed by running or lifting weights. I admit I took pride in the amount of weight I could bench press and the large amount of weight I could leg press.

On my first visit to physical therapy, the therapist put a towel on the floor. I sat at a low table, and she asked if I was able to move the towel with my leg. I thought it was laughable. Who couldn't move a towel across the floor? I put my foot down on the towel, pulled, and then pushed with all I had, but couldn't budge it. After taking a break, the therapist asked me to lie down on the table. She put a five-pound weight on my legs and asked me to lift my leg. I gave it my best effort, to no avail. It slowly began to set in that this was going to be a difficult and long journey. I could only walk a short distance on crutches before the pain overwhelmed me to the point of being nauseated. It took months to learn how to walk.

By the end of 1983, after additional surgeries and daily physical therapy, I was able to walk on crutches throughout the house without a lot of pain. My right ankle and leg continued to be troublesome spots. After a lot of consultation and seeing some of the top orthopedic surgeons, the decision was made to fuse my right ankle using some of the bone from my fibula. Little did we know we were about to face one of the most trying times in our young lives. In January 1984, doctors performed a fusion with a rod going up through my heel and into my tibia. A hole was made in the bottom of the cast for the rod. It extended from the bottom of my foot about four inches.

In February, the pin and cast were still in place from the fusion. One night, my family drove to a restaurant in San Antonio just to get away for the evening. Not more than 15 minutes into the hour-long trip, everyone began complaining about an awful smell in the car. It was my cast. I knew the cast had developed a bad smell but wasn't aware of how overpowering the smell was until my family's comments. By the time we reached San

Antonio, everyone was ready to get out of the car and into fresh air. The complaints grew louder on the return trip home. I was almost left on the side of the road! Once we reached home, my family insisted I call the doctor first thing the next morning. That was a long night because of fear and anxiety. I knew the odds were that I had a severe bone infection. The pain started during the night, and I felt like my leg was on fire.

I called the doctor and told him about the odor. He insisted that I come in immediately. My dad drove me to the orthopedic doctor's office, where we were taken back to an examination room immediately upon arrival. The surgeon removed a portion of the cast at the incision site near my ankle. Both the recent and past incisions had opened due to infection. There was a horrible odor and drainage from all the places the skin had opened from the swelling. The surgeon then removed another area of the cast near the pin where there was a large amount of drainage. The doctor left the room without saying anything and returned with a pair of pliers. My dad realized what the doctor was about to do and laid across me to hold me down. It felt like a hot iron had gone through my leg as the doctor pulled the pin from the bone. He then explained the mistake of waiting 24 hours from the time I noticed an odor until I contacted his office. The pin tract was badly infected, and time was of the essence.

He ordered I go immediately to the hospital and said he would perform surgery as soon as the hospital staff prepped me. He would attempt to clean out the infection. By the time the doctor arrived, I was running a high fever. The doctor decided to start antibiotics but delay the surgery. After further testing and additional x-rays, the medical staff told me the odds were very high they would need to perform an amputation because of the infection. I was admitted to a "step down area" which was located next to the ICU. Over the next week, I received various IV antibiotics and the regular daily pin tract cleaning. This painful process involved the nurses using long swabs to clean out the pin tract and the areas that had burst open. The wound cleaning was a dreaded, but necessary task. For the next 18 days, they ran swabs through my heel into my tibia for a culture of the infection. Every morning, we heard doctors discussing the severity of the infection outside my hospital room. I would lie in my hospital bed during those 18 days and wonder when doctors would tell me I needed an amputation because of the spreading infection. But each day, they said I could keep my leg another 24 hours without amputating. My wife was with me as much as she could during the day and often spent the night. Brandon stayed with my parents. Many people prayed and believed that God would spare my life again and an amputation wouldn't be necessary.

On the 19th day, the doctor walked in with a good report. "I can't explain it," he said. "That was one of the worst infections I've seen, but amputation is no longer being considered."

My leg started healing at a rapid rate. I'm not sure why God didn't heal the first day we prayed, but He brought the infection under control and spared my life once again. Often, when we pray and God answers immediately, we quickly move ahead without giving much thought to what God has done for us. We appreciate the miracle more when God delays. We realize it was truly a miracle and not a result of man's efforts.

I was kept in the hospital for an additional week for the wounds to heal and to receive additional antibiotics. In just a few days, we went from being fearful of the unknown to having wheelchair races in the hospital hallway with my brother!

> I was learning to stop and thank God for what He was doing in my life. My wife and I also were learning that we could tell people about God's work in our lives and bring encouragement to them. Through sharing our testimony, we told others about the grace of God and how we could take our concerns to God with an expectation He would answer our prayer. I'm thankful for those who operate in the spiritual gifts, but I'm even more thankful that someone like me can pray with expectation. God knows me, hears me, and is concerned about my needs. Often, those who face great difficulty compare their trials to the ones Job faced in the Bible. The Bible tells us God handpicked Job because of his consistent walk of faith. I did not have Job's consistency in my daily walk and I was far from Job's level of devotion.

"What is man that You are mindful of him, And the son of man that You visit him? 5 For You have made him a little lower than the angels, And You have crowned him with glory and honor. 6 You have made him to have dominion over the works of Your hands; You have put all things under his feet." (Psalm 8:4- 6)

There are no qualifiers, such as I must have served God for a certain amount of time or even be a licensed minister. I realize this passage is prophetic about the coming of the Messiah. He was born, died, and arose on the third day. We now have dominion over every tool of the enemy. Jesus Christ put all things under His feet. As His child, I too can put fear, doubt, anxiety, depression, and oppression under my feet. I do not have to live constantly in fear of what my future holds. One of the most amazing things I've personally witnessed is a dear saint of God lying on his death bed, knowing his life was measured in minutes and not years. He had a smile on his face and a peace no medication can bring. I've watched on more than one occasion as children of God took their final breaths with joy in their hearts and a peace that only comes from knowing they have dominion over death. They may not live in this world for long, but they soon will cross into a land where there is no death, tears, or sorrow.

Instead of feeling like Job, who was chosen for his righteousness, I often have felt like the man in Mark 9 who came to Jesus because his child was possessed with a spirit. This man told of the horrific torment his son faced. He gnashed at people when they walked by and threw himself into the fire. But when the man got to Jesus and asked Him to deliver his son, Jesus says, "if you can believe, all things are possible to him that believeth." This man makes a simple statement, "I believe, but Lord, help my unbelief." The scripture says "straightway" the boy is set free.

We all have scars from the past that can keep us from believing God loves us and desires the best for us. My wife and I learned we could bind together with an expectation God would hear our simple prayers. We've not always prayed a boisterous prayer, but we've often held hands in a doctor's office or a hospital room, quietly asking God to intervene again. We had seen God work in the past, so we expected that somehow God would answer.

One of the interesting parts of the story in Mark 9 is when Jesus asked the man how long his son had faced torment. The father answered, "since he was a child." When he put his son in the hands of Jesus, his son was immediately healed. Too often, we put up with issues in our lives that could have been left behind if we had only asked the Lord to help our unbelief. I wrestle with things when I put issues in God's hands and then remove them because I feel He isn't working fast enough or working how I think He should. I feel I'm making some headway because I stubbornly massage it, worry over it, and lose sleep over it, but really it is just making the issue last much longer than it should. If the man in Mark 9 had put his son in the hands of Jesus earlier, the boy's years of torment would have been shortened.

I'm impatient and like to get disorderly things back in order as quickly as possible. I wonder how often God would like to ask me, "How long have you dealt with this?" It's not because He doesn't have the answer, but as a way of reminding me it easily could have been left in the past if I had given it to Him and said, "LORD, I BELIEVE all things are possible." I slowly learned to put it all in His hands. My wife and I learned there was no other alternative. Our only hope was in God. As we saw God work time after time, opening doors for my health issues, our finances, and our children's lives, we began to step out by faith and expand our prayers. We went from praying just for my health to praying and placing our finances in the hands of God. It amazed us how God provided and made a way in every area of our lives. We prayed for our children's mental health because they saw me go through pain and watched as I was placed in the hospital or had to experience surgery after surgery.

Brandon's second grade teacher called one day to let me know that he failed a spelling test. I couldn't understand why he failed the test because he knew how to spell all the words on the list when I helped him study. His explanation didn't make a lot of sense. His teacher and I discovered that Brandon hadn't brought home the new spelling list for the past few weeks because he didn't want to bother us. I had been in the hospital. He felt badly, even at a very early age, about asking us to help him with a new spelling list. Both of our sons tried to minimize their problems because they knew I faced such big challenges. We tried not to discuss my health issues in front of them but there was no hiding from them what I was going through. Overall, it was the life they both grew up knowing. They were forced to deal with our family's situation at times. Prayer for our sons became a big part of our prayer life. When they were in high school, I often went in their rooms during the night and prayed God would keep them and watch over them and their convictions would be strong.

We prayed for things such as our home appliances when they broke down. We prayed for our car when it had mechanical difficulties. We prayed for every issue that arose because we saw God somehow provided in each situation. The washer or dryer might not have been immediately repaired, but God would connect us with someone who could make the repair or provide us the finances to pay for the repairs. We found God's ways are truly above our ways. He has provided for our every need.

Throughout the 1980s, I logged at least three to four major surgeries a year and many other day surgeries. There always seemed to be pins or other hardware that needed to be removed or other procedures that needed to be performed. We would schedule the next surgery while recovering from a previous surgery. I experienced additional infections and other complications almost yearly. By this time, I had been referred to a long list of highly skilled specialists. There were neurologists for the nerve damage in my arms, hands, and back. I had orthopedic surgeons for just about every major joint in my body. The main orthopedic surgeon, Dr. Smoot, oversaw all my orthopedic needs. He specialized in lower extremities. He fused joints in my foot using bone from my hips. Time and again the joints failed to fuse because sometimes I went against doctor's orders and walked too soon. Most times, there was simply no explanation. After one attempt to re-fuse a joint in my foot, small pieces of bone crumbled onto the surgical instruments. We reached a point when surgeons used cadaver bones because too much bone had been taken from my hips and other areas. Bones from my left ankle crumbled and grew into painful bone spurs. I also suffered from numerous serious back injuries. I felt like I spent more time in the hospital than out.

My wife gave birth to Christopher in January 1988. By this time, pain management doctors started emerging on the medical scene across the country. I was one of the first pain management patients in Austin. My patient number was 34. I'm not against taking medication, but it was clear this doctor's goal was to give as much pain medicine as I could take and remain alive. Little thought was given to my quality of life. I had no desire to be on major medications the rest of my life. I feared addiction and knew it would take increased dosages to control the pain as time went on.

Surgeries began to pile up in the late 1980s. When I visited a new doctor's office, I simply wrote "too many to list" when asked on the medical form to list all my surgeries. The surgeries started taking a mental toll. My nightmares became more prevalent, and my anxiety grew worse in the days leading up to surgery. I slept little and paced the floor the night before surgery. I thought my anxiety would lessen with the additional procedures, but it increased. Some years later, a counselor explained that while the conscious can be put to sleep with anesthesia, the subconscious stays awake and says, "here comes that guy in scrubs with a knife and he is going to cut on me and it will hurt." I also knew little could be done about the severe pain I would feel after surgery. The surgeons did their best to delay the onset of the harsh pain by using local anesthetics at the surgery site, but that wears off.

Since almost all my surgeries were at the same hospital, I came to know most of the anesthesiologists. They knew how anxious I would get. After one of my surgeries, the chief anesthesiologist told me her anesthesiology group would pay for dental work to repair my front teeth which chipped after I chomped down on the intubation tube as I went to sleep. I hadn't noticed until she mentioned it. When I ran my tongue over my two top front teeth, I could feel the rough edge of chipped teeth and one badly cracked tooth. I was told that I sat up and fought the nursing staff as I was waking up. I don't remember any of this, but I was embarrassed at what happened. My teeth were repaired a few weeks after the surgery, but I chipped my teeth again just days later when I had another orthopedic surgery. After I chipped and cracked my teeth a third time, the same chief of anesthesiology informed me that I would be put to sleep gradually for all my future surgeries. While I waited in the pre-operation area, doctors gave me medication that put me out before getting to the operating room and they would allow me to wake up more slowly and naturally.

Even now, I still get extremely nervous leading up to any procedure, major or small. It isn't unusual for my blood pressure to be in the range of 200/180 when I check into the hospital for surgery. I've been blessed to have my pastor, Rodney Shaw, come to pray before many of my surgeries. It always helps. I take my iPhone or iPad and my headphones to the pre-op area. The anesthesiologist and nurses know having my wife with me until the last second is one of the best sedatives, so they want her there with me. When she stands up and gives me a kiss, I know she has gotten the nod from the anesthesiologist and I will be asleep before I arrive in the operating room.

Philippians 4:6-7 tells us to *"be careful for nothing; but in everything by prayer and supplication with thanksgiving let your request be made known unto God. And the peace of God which passeth all understanding shall keep your hearts and minds through Christ Jesus."* There are some storms we must go through. There are some trials we will face on earth. In the trial, "prayer and supplication" come easily, but I don't always let my request be made known with thanksgiving in the middle of the trial. Paul said the peace that passes all understanding comes when we make our requests known to God with thanksgiving.

Our prayer before surgery has become, "God, we thank You in advance for moving on the doctors and making them the best surgeons they've ever been. We thank You in advance for helping us with the pain and for bringing us through another surgery and for the rest and comfort that You will give us tonight." When I make my requests known to Him with thanksgiving, there is a peace that passes all understanding that comes in and gives comfort to me and my wife. I still get anxious. I still get restless the night before surgery, but I roam around the house less.

Pamala and I pray with thanksgiving before we do anything. Before traveling, we pray, "Thank You, God, for a safe trip. Thank You, God, for keeping your hand on us and for watching over us and keeping us safe as we travel." A year ago, we prayed this prayer while sitting in the car in our driveway just before leaving on a five-hour drive to northeast Texas. We were running behind. In a rush to load the car and double check to see if we had everything, we failed to pray before walking out of the house. Before putting the car in reverse, Pamala said, "We didn't pray!" While sitting in our car, we thanked Him for His grace and mercy and for keeping His hand on us as we traveled. We were about 60 miles from our destination when several 18-wheelers backed up traffic. Once we got a few miles out of that town, a pickup truck crossed into our lane, hit the car in front of us head on, and killed the driver instantly. God had protected us!

Making my requests known to God with thanksgiving will bring His peace and protection. Paul told us in II Corinthians 12:10 that "When I am weak, then I am strong." It's not necessary to "tough out" every situation. I become strong when I share my weak moments and anxieties with God. I always like to put on a good front and act strong to those around me, but God knows what I am experiencing. If I thank God for victory and peace in advance, He strengthens, comforts, wraps His arms around me, and lets me know I am not forgotten.

31

Chapter 6

NEW TECHNIQUES

In the early 1990s, I began experiencing far more severe back pain than ever before. My wife rushed me to the emergency room due to extreme pain on several occasions. We would stay in the hospital three to four days to get the pain under control. Many times, we would leave the hospital only to return the same evening. On one hospital visit, my neurologist talked to me about a new program for trauma patients who were willing to try less medication while learning newly developed techniques to tolerate constant pain. The program accepted only five people per week. It required patients to have a high pain tolerance and be willing to stay three weeks without pain medication of any type. I reluctantly agreed to take the written test required to be put on the list.

The test helped medical staff determine patients' personality type. This would prove beneficial later. I met the criteria and was taken by ambulance to the rehabilitation center where I checked in and kissed my wife goodbye. I could only see her once a day, from 5 to 6 p.m. Phone calls were only allowed from

5 to 8 p.m. One patient was a young lady who experienced trauma after an 18-wheeler crashed into her while driving her new car for the first time on the freeway. Another patient was an attorney who was shot at point-blank range while representing a woman in a divorce case. The soon-to-be ex-husband walked into the attorney's office, shot him multiple

times, and injured his spinal cord and internal organs. Another was a lady who had been held prisoner in the "killing fields" of Vietnam and was brutally beaten and abused until she escaped and was able to make her way to the United States. She had gone to work and suffered an additional injury on the job. We all were barely able to walk and suffered PTSD as well as bodily injuries.

Patients in the program awakened daily at 5 a.m. to eat a breakfast designed specifically for each person. At 6 a.m., we started a rigorous exercise program. Pool workouts were followed by other physical tasks and lessons on how to do various household tasks such as loading the dryer, washing machine or dishwasher without stressing our body. The day was interspersed with short private counseling sessions. Then came physical therapists, nurses, doctors, and pain management counselors who oversaw our every move. Lunch and dinner were also specifically designed for each person. After dinner each evening, we were taken to a shopping area or a restaurant and shown how to get in and out of the car, in and out of the place of business, and how to sit or stand so we would be in less pain. The medical team took various types of pillows, supports, canes, walkers, and other devices for us to get a feel for what worked the best. We all vowed to revolt together and leave the first week, but we decided to stick it out. All five of us completed the three-week program. By the second week, we were in somewhat of a routine and seeing some improvement. This encouraged us to push forward and do more each day.

Staff added more to the regimen and greatly increased our level of exercise in the second week. It was more than any of us imagined we could ever achieve. The swimming exercise went from walking in the water to spending an hour swimming laps and treading water for up to 15 minutes or more. The staff who traveled with us during our evening outings worked with us using various pillows to help us be more comfortable in our chairs or while traveling in the car. They helped us with specific walkers or canes to get to and from the van. The program's aim was to wean us from any device that was not an absolute necessity. We were given no pain medication, other than utilizing a cold spray on the areas hurting the most.

We received encouragement from the counselors and physical therapists. We had three daily private counseling sessions ranging from 15 minutes to 45 minutes. We also did an hour of stretching that enhanced our movement. Each Friday, we individually met the entire staff. The staff was encouraging, but honest about what we had and hadn't achieved that week. They let us know if we didn't push and work as hard as possible, we would find ourselves limited in the years to come.

My group felt like we had greatly improved by the time the third and final week arrived. Our diet was still the chief discussion. We had our own small area where we were served specific meals designed specifically for each patient. We were watched as we ate, so there was no food traded among us. The meal was designed to aid in our healing. It had very little seasoning of any kind and was food I would never order in a restaurant. I knew I would still get hungry between meals even if I ate everything on my plate. I developed a game plan to down every morsel of food on my plate. I started with the food item I disliked the most and moved my way to the food I could at least tolerate. This ended my meal in a somewhat positive experience.

On Thursday of the final week, we were videoed walking across the room and doing a few other tasks. We then watched the videos of us walking on that first day prior to any therapy and then the videos that were just shot. We were all amazed at the massive and undeniable improvements we saw. By the third week, I had improved to the point I could sneak over to the adjoining hospital gift shop and load up on snacks after the 8:30 p.m. bed check.

The last day, the entire staff met with us individually and explained the positives they saw and what they felt we could achieve if we kept working. We were glad we stuck in there and didn't quit the first week. I still use many of the methods and tools we were taught during that three-week period. Though not intended to be spiritual in nature, many of the disciplines the staff taught had some biblical truths.

Job said, "the thing I feared has come upon me." The Bible is clear about the power of the spoken word and how our subconscious retains what we've spoken. In that program, the staff closely listened to the things we said and observed what we did. If we used a phrase such as "my back is killing me," we were stopped immediately and asked if we were really dying. If so, they would take us to the hospital. If not, they asked us to quit using those kinds of phrases. It was fine to describe pain as burning, stabbing, sharp or dull, but we were to exercise caution in how we stated our complaints. The subconscious will hold what we've stated in our mind and soon can make the pain worse.

God still had not given me total healing, but He placed me at the right place with the right people so I could be part of an extremely helpful program. The staff brought improvement to my life and greatly aided in my quality of living. I gained mental tools to assist in dealing with the pain that remained in my back.

Chapter 7

SET BACK

Anyone who has spent any time around a doctor's office or hospital has witnessed great technological advances. I experienced months in the hospital with pain medication given intramuscular (IM) instead of intravenously (IV), as is done today. One problem with intramuscular injections is that large knots formed from the medication. By the end of the first few years, I had permanent knots in my hips, thighs, arms, and other injection sites. The knots became an issue over time. In the late 1980s and early 1990s, I was having surgeries on my ankles, feet, and legs and was in and out of the hospital for non-surgical treatment of pain. Medication was injected into my legs and hips. Muscles in the upper leg are large and can absorb the medication easily.

We had been out of the hospital for only a few days when I realized my left leg had become sore, red, and slowly filling with fluid in a small area. Another emergency room trip revealed infection, which led to another surgery to clean it. Doctors removed a large area of muscle, four inches by four inches, down to the bone and left the area open to heal from the inside out. There was a lot of fluid in the muscle and along my thigh bone where they tunneled along the bone to remove the infected tissue and muscle.

Throughout the night, nursing staff replaced my blood-saturated bedding every few hours. Early the next morning, I left a trail of blood in the hallway as nurses pushed me in a wheelchair to a whirlpool tub. The water in the tub turned red from the blood loss. The doctor determined I needed another surgery to stop the bleeding. Additional images showed infection still along the bone. I experienced far less bleeding after this surgery, but the doctor said I needed a blood transfusion. This was at a time when HIV and hepatitis were a concern. My wife donated blood along with my father, my two wonderful siblings, and a family friend who was over 80 years old at the time. The friend's blood and my wife's blood proved to be the best match.

A team of nurses cleaned the wound and replaced the bandages several times a day. This was especially painful. The bandages were placed in a solution of saline and medications, then pushed into the tunnel along the femur before large gauze squares were placed into the hole. The bandages stuck to the sides of the wound when they dried, pulling newly formed skin each time the gauze was removed. This stopped the wound from forming a scab and had to be replaced several times a day. My wife learned the procedure so she could do the same thing at home. She called my dad to assist her in changing the bandages on the first day home. I tried to hide the pain from it, but it was no use. I realized caregivers have it more difficult than patients. On many occasions, I look at my wife, who is less than 5 feet tall, and see her as a giant in moments like these.

Chapter 8

THE CAREGIVER

Pamala knew little about my hobbies when I met her. She has one sibling, a younger sister. Her father did not enjoy fishing, hunting, sports, or most of the things I did on a routine basis. Fishing and hunting were things everyone did in Kilgore, where I was raised. Both of my grandparents loved to fish and camp. One of my grandfathers bought a new boat and no longer used his much older aluminum boat. After a little work, I got the old boat running and the trailer back in shape. My grandfather helped me weld a trailer hitch onto my car so I could pull the boat and be on the lake fishing in just a few minutes. I hunted with an elderly man in the church who often didn't take a gun. He just enjoyed being in the woods. I cleaned whatever I caught, tossed it in the freezer, and my mom would cook it for dinner. When I married Pamala, I continued to do the same thing, but my wife balked at cooking my wild game. When she pulled out a plastic bag with a clean and skinned squirrel inside, she screamed and emphatically stated, "In no way am I touching this!" I loved to go squirrel hunting and loved dumplings made with squirrel meat. Pamala overcame her fear and learned to cook everything, including fish, venison, and squirrel.

After my accident, Pamala faced the caregiver role much the same way. She balked at times, but in the end, she took on needed tasks and saw them through. Only one time did she ever get squeamish. That moment came when a surgeon removed over 50 large staples from two large incisions. I noticed the nurse observing my wife. The nurse asked if she needed a seat and then reached to grab her as she fell slowly to the floor. She recovered by the time we left.

Pamala has slept on all types of benches, sofas, chairs, and a sundry of other places to be by my side. She sat for untold hours in surgical waiting areas, doctors' offices, and labs because she knew I wanted her nearby. The caregiver's role is lonely at times. Caregivers often know more than the patient about the challenges the patient faces. They are worn and tired, functioning on little sleep and a diet of fast food. The medical staff does not ask caregivers how they are doing because all the focus is on the patient. I've often said I'm given medication and go to sleep while she sits awake, still concerned about the surgery or the latest update from the doctors or nursing staff. The caregiver's role is one of the most important in the life of a patient. My wife has filled the caregiver's role as well as anyone could have filled this vital role.

We were talking about purchasing a home when I went into the hospital. She found a great home and made the decision to buy it without me seeing it. The best she could do was to show me a few photos. She brought the contract to my hospital room for me to sign after she had negotiated the deal. I did not see the home until a few days before our closing date.

She leased another home and I saw it as we were getting ready to move into it. She would video our sons' sporting events so I wouldn't miss out completely. I honestly don't know how she was able to be a wonderful mom and caregiver all at the same time. No matter how badly I felt, I knew when she arrived at my hospital room each evening, everything would be okay. On many occasions, I'd be in a hospital bed in pain without knowing Pamala was going to arrive. When my ears heard the distinct clicking of her heels on the tile floor, an instant peace flooded me. I felt guilty that she came to the hospital after working, taking care of the boys and other tasks, but I was so happy she came. I was told that I called her name in my sleep on more than one occasion. I am thankful God saw what I would face long before we even married. I am so grateful that He put a strong, determined woman in my life. I would not be here today without her.

The early MRI machines were much smaller than those today. The scans are difficult for me due to claustrophobia and my back pain. It isn't unusual for me to have three to four MRIs a year. One of my physicians ordered an MRI and I was told it had to been done immediately. The longer I sat in the waiting area, the worse my anxiety became. Pamala talked the staff into letting her into the room with me during my procedure. I put on the hospital gown, got on the small table that slides into the tube, and began to feel the tightness of the narrow tunnel. They started the machine and heard the familiar loud knocking that takes place every few minutes. I had a burning, stabbing back pain. The technician told me I was starting to move too much. Pamala stepped to the tube and began patting and rubbing my shin while singing words from an old hymn.

"Peace, peace, wonderful peace," she sang. "Coming down from the Father above. Sweep over my spirit, forever I pray, in fathomless billows of love."

Her soothing touch and soft voice took my mind off the experience for the next 45 minutes. She brought me peace and ushered the love of God into the room. We both felt relaxed and at ease. I was no longer concerned with the impending results. My caregiver brought peace, comfort, and encouragement like no drug or any other thing on this earth. We walked out knowing she had once again risen to the moment and helped me get through a difficult time.

Another time wasn't as trying for me, but greatly embarrassing for her. The doctor prescribed Xanax for me to take "about the time we leave our home." I took the small pill as ordered. Upon arrival, the radiologist informed us the doctor had ordered me to take two pills when we got there and not just the one pill at home. I was extremely anxious and in pain and wasn't going to argue with the doctor. I took two more Xanax and felt nothing from it. The pills were having zero effect, or at least that's what I thought. I stepped into a changing room, locked the door behind me, and took off my clothes to put on a gown for the MRI. I don't remember anything else after that. I was found sitting down in the changing room, sound asleep with my clothing folded neatly next to me. They woke me up to get in the MRI machine. I snored so much that it caused me to move, and they couldn't complete the MRI.

It is easy to try to keep things from one another. I've laid in bed thinking, "I can't wake my wife until morning." Somehow, I hold on so she can sleep. Caregivers know what they will face next. There are times medical personnel have given her a negative report that she kept to herself until things improved. Only then would she tell me how dire the situation had been. Keeping secrets can lead to distrust. It is best to keep communication open. So often you see a couple in a restaurant, both on their phones, not speaking to each other while they are out for the evening. We didn't have any such devices in the 1980s when I had my accident. We were early in our marriage and were forced to sit in a hospital room for days on end. We learned how to communicate. Otherwise, we would go crazy. I had to learn that she needed time to get away from the hospital and doctors, and yes, even me, though I hated to see her go. She learned I wanted her there with me, not always to talk but just be there by my side quietly. The caregiver role is one I don't envy but I'm extremely thankful I married a lady who is giving and caring in every way.

I suffered most when Pamala battled a physical challenge such as Bell's Palsy which caused her face to be drawn on the side. She suffered off and on from migraines, but Bell's Palsy created anxiety and concerns about hampering her efforts to care for her family. In one church service, she walked to the front for prayer. Others came forward to pray for her before she returned to her seat unchanged. Our sons said, "NO mom, you are going back for prayer until you get your healing." They were still young but knew the power of prayer.

She returned to the altar determined to receive her healing. This time, she returned to her seat with a noticeable change in her face. The Bells Palsy left her. Her face and facial features relaxed and returned to normal. I believe she received her healing because she refused anything less than total healing. Her second trip to the altar showed a level of faith above the norm. It reminded me of the blind man who saw men as trees walking. When he prayed a second time, God healed him. I know it sounds a bit selfish to say I needed her whole. Since my accident, I have a sensitivity to my family not being well. There are times my family thought I was angry because of the way I acted when they got sick or injured. I wasn't angry, but I struggled seeing them in pain or sickness. I simply can't watch or read anything about someone's suffering.

I stopped hunting because it was too difficult to see an animal die. I am more compassionate than I was before my accident. However, it bothers me when my family refrains from telling me about their own illnesses or injuries. They deem their pain insignificant compared to my health battles. My sons would not tell me about their injuries or illnesses when they were in high school. My wife has also kept health issues from me. I would rather them tell me so I can return the care they've given me. I still have some of the old "tough-it-out" mentality in me. Most people who know me will say I don't complain a lot. I rarely tell people about my accident unless they ask. It isn't unusual to be at the pharmacy where people will share their experience with slings, crutches or walking boots when they see me outfitted in one of them. People will sometimes go into detail and drone on about their own injuries. If the complaining seems like it will never end, I will eventually say, "I fell from a five-story building and had X number of surgeries." That usually ends the conversation! If they say something along the line of "I hope you aren't like me. I've had two surgeries on my ankle and had to be on crutches both times," I let it go and tell them I'm sorry they've had to experience that. It is when I'm on crutches and someone with a minor injury is using an automated shopping cart and tells me how horrible his sprain is or how he fell and had to wear a cast for four weeks, that I can't help myself and I tell them a few of my experiences.

Chapter 9

HEALED!

Over a period of several months, I felt violent pain in my shoulders and elbows for seconds if I sneezed or coughed. The pain would then fade away, leaving badly aching joints. This pain grew worse. Every time I strained, I felt intense pain in the same places. The neurosurgeon performed a brief exam and then ordered an MRI. Between my visit to the neurosurgeon and getting the MRI results, I had to be admitted to the hospital every few days to get control of the pain. By this time, we were well known at Seton hospital, a large, well-respected hospital in Austin. We were so well known that we were often given a large suite if one was available. The attendant on staff would have a hamburger and Dr. Pepper waiting in my room.

When the day came for us to get the results, the neurologist felt like he knew the problem but insisted I get a second opinion from another neurosurgeon, Dr. John Calverley, chief of neurosurgery at the University of Texas Galveston Medical Branch. He was known for his long career in dealing with difficult neuro-related issues. He was also known for being personable with his patients. Many of my Austin physicians studied under Dr. Calverley while attending medical school during their neurosurgery rotation. He was listed in *Town and Country Magazine's* list of "Outstanding American Medical Specialists" three times and received the Texas Neurological Society Lifetime Achievement Award in 2004.

We were taken to Dr. Calverley's office instead of an examination room, which I thought was odd at the time. After being reassured by the nursing staff that Dr. Calverley would be with us shortly, and once again told how beloved he was by his patients, Dr. Calverley came into the office with a bounding stride, sat down at his desk, and asked me to describe what I was experiencing. He had copies of the MRIs taken in Austin and said, "if it walks like a duck, and quacks like a duck, it is usually a duck." He added that he would explore all possibilities. Dr. Calverley called in the chief of radiology to view my MRIs without giving the radiologist any information about what I was experiencing or my accident. The radiologist instantly said, "It's obvious this man has a tumor growing inside his spinal cord the size of the average man's forefinger, but there must be an additional issue because you wouldn't call me in for something so easily detected."

Dr Calverley let us know this was exactly what my doctors in Austin had seen. It was what he expected when hearing of my symptoms. He was not surprised when he saw the imaging results. The only thing left at this point would be to make plans for him to go inside my spinal cord to remove the growth. There is an odd relief when you finally discover what is causing the issues. You pray for nothing to be wrong but can be frustrated when nothing is found. No one hopes for a serious medical issue to be discovered, but you know when something is wrong and needs to be addressed. Dr. Calverley had seen similar patients with this type of growth in their spinal cord some years after traumatic accidents like mine. He made clear it had to be more than a car wreck or other type crash, but a massive jolt such as one would experience from a high-level fall. If he didn't remove the growth, it would likely continue down my spinal cord causing more trauma. The plan was to return to Austin for additional MRIs, since these were now over a month old, and return for the surgery to open my spinal cord and remove the tumor. He explained that the spinal cord expands for an instant with pressure such as a cough or sneeze. Pressure on the tumor was what I was feeling in my elbows and shoulders. Though it was a serious operation, he felt we had no other option but to remove the growth as quickly as possible.

We returned home for the needed medical tests, and all the while praying God's hand be on us. We learned to pray for all the medical personnel as well. We prayed that God would enable them to have great insight and be the best medical staff they could be. We returned to UT Galveston ready for the surgery. At this time, the hospital was one of the main hospitals used for the Texas prison system. While waiting on the elevator to ride up to Dr. Calverley's office, the elevator door opened to a man whose hands and feet were chained to his wheelchair, his head shaved with a large bandage on his skull and in prison clothes. He had Texas Department of Safety officers around him. This did little to put my wife at ease on the way to Dr. Calverley's office. Once we arrived at our floor, and the color came back to my wife's face from our elevator ride, little was said between the two of us. We were greatly concerned about the seriousness of the coming days. We've somewhat learned to recognize how serious an issue is by how the nursing staff gives you that certain look of pity. I am aware they see all types of diseases and sickness daily, but the human condition still allows for the average person to have a level of concern that can't be easily hidden. We saw this in the nurses' eyes who had taken us to the doctor's office.

When Dr. Calverley entered the room, he asked that we follow him to view the MRIs in a large room with lighted boards all around the room. He showed us the first set of MRIs and pointed out what was clearly the tumor. It looked like a black line to me, but it was easily seen. He then pointed to the latest MRIs.

"In the first set of MRIs, you can clearly see the tumor and how large it was," Dr. Calverley said. "Now look at the latest MRI results, and you'll see there is no sign of the tumor."

Dr. Calverley called the same chief of radiology and asked him to view the second set of images. He also agreed the tumor was in the first set but not the second set.

"Remember when I said if it walks like a duck, and quacks like a duck, it must be a duck?" the doctor asked. My wife and I nodded in unison. He said my symptoms were classic textbook symptoms for the type of tumor the first images revealed. He said my case would typically be a great lesson for medical students on the classic symptoms and complications patients face from such. But with joy, he explained that now there was no tumor in the imaging. After some additional testing, he decided not to even admit us to the hospital or perform an operation. We rejoiced all the way home for another miracle God performed in our lives! Though the pain in my elbow and shoulders took many months to go away, and I would have major back issues in the future, we avoided complicated surgery. God did the work even if the pain continued. There was clear evidence that what was once visible was now no longer there. We told Dr. Calverley that we and our church prayed for the miraculous. He simply said he had no explanation for what he saw. I know God heals.

> Faith is necessary, but I don't believe faith means the removal of all doubt. I'm glad that simply saying "Lord, I believe, but help my unbelief" is enough. I have too often prayed with more questions than answers and with great anxiety and fear, but my asking for God's hand to work in my life is a sign of faith. The Bible tells us that we are each given a "measure" of faith. I've often thought that the measure varied depending on my situation but having enough faith to quote the first four words of Genesis 1:1, "In the beginning, God...," is all the faith I need. God was there from the very beginning. He created me. If He created me, then there is no one better to repair me. I believe prayer safeguards my mind. There is no greater battlefield for Satan than our minds.
>
> My prayers for God to guard my mind and help me fight has given me the ability to have a far greater quality of life than any physician predicted over the last 40+ years. I want God to push out thoughts that He isn't interested in my plight. I want Him to erase thoughts that He will not hear or answer my prayers if I fail to pray or hold to spiritual disciplines. Of course, that is no excuse for not holding to the disciplines, but there are times I've failed to pray or read the Bible as much as I should. I got busy with doctor appointments and life. I ask for God's forgiveness and help to get me back on track. He understands when I am sincere.

I ask for God to guard my mind from always fearing the worst. I am still learning every pain doesn't equate to a serious issue. I'm learning to place my cares on the Lord. I often get consumed researching every detail from my doctor visits. Now that doctors use apps that allow you to see their notes, it can be easy to get caught up in every word written and what they may mean, especially when it comes to lab results. My wife will ask me why I worry when I can't do anything about it. I realize I am not a doctor, and I can do little about the issue, but my nature is to research every lab report and comb through apps like "My Chart" to view the doctor's summary. They can be a great tool, but they can also provide the enemy with an entrance to your thoughts. Paul encouraged us in Philippians 4:8 to "think on whatsoever things are true, honest, just, pure, lovely, of a good report and if there be any virtue and if there be any praise, think on these things."

If I'm not careful, I can dwell on the wrong things and find myself filled with stress, worry, doubt, and fear. No matter what I am facing, I have much for which to give praise, even in my times of great struggle. I should have died at a young age, but instead I've been blessed with at least 40 additional years. I have lived to see two sons grow up and marry. I have five grandchildren and have been blessed with the greatest wife in the world. Though my wife and I have spent wedding anniversaries, birthdays, and every major holiday in the hospital at some point, I still have much to think about that is pure, lovely, and of a good report. I praise God for those things daily. When I am discouraged and in the darkest of days, I think about these things. When I dwell on the many blessings in my life, I start to walk out of the dark into the light of the Lord. That in no way means I bury my head in the sand and forget my health struggles. I wake up every few hours each night due to pain across my body. I haven't slept one single night all the way through since October 1982. I still have the same nightmare I had after my accident as we prepare for each surgery. I limp and can't do many of the things I wish I could do. I also know that I will face more surgeries in the future. I have no idea what lies ahead, but when I can think on the good things of God and list His blessings in my life, I cannot help but to feel the load grow lighter. My faith rises and I feel the peace that goes beyond all understanding. All it takes is my saying, "God, I thank You for giving me Your name that is above every name. I thank You for forgiving me of my sins. Thank You for filling me with Your spirit and for blessing me with life and health." Yes, I still thank God for health. Each day I get to visit with family, children, and grandchildren is a great day. Each day I can kiss my wife good morning is a blessed day. I cannot forget to think about these things.

Many with long-term medical challenges will eventually take one of two roads. Some take as much pain medication as they can get, curl up in bed and feel sorry for themselves. Some fight. Fighters still require some type of pain management, but they tend to navigate their situation better. Fighters tend to exercise more, keep a good daily diet, and strive to live as normal a life as possible. Some surgeries which once required long periods of physical therapy, no longer have physical therapy prescribed whatsoever. Patients who exercise daily after physical therapy do well. Those who don't, quickly lose all they gained during the period of physical therapy.

For my first of three knee replacements, my doctors ordered weeks of physical therapy. With the help of God and a made-up mind, I worked through the pain to gain as much movement as possible. By the time I arrived at physical therapy, I had far exceeded the range of motion that therapists would work to gain. A few weeks of exercise is all that was needed to strengthen the areas that had not been used from the degeneration of my knee.

I am a horrible patient who lacks patience. I have caused myself additional trouble a few times. On one such occasion, I hobbled too fast on crutches across a wet, slippery parking lot only to go crashing to the pavement after one physical therapy session. I knocked a pin out of the bone in my leg and through the skin. That landed me back in the hospital operating room.

It seems as if my wife and I fight one battle, and before we can catch our breath, we face another. The onset of one battle occurred when doctors decided to implant a pain pump, a simple outpatient procedure in which the catheter is fully implanted while a computer device that regulates the medication is left externally for 10 days. A small amount of medication is needed since the catheter goes to the spinal cord and the medication bathes the spinal nerves. The pain pump is worn for a week to 10 days. During this time,the computer device is worn around the waist with an alarm that sounds to warn that the catheter is being closed off or having other issues. I tried to preach with the device around my waist. As I preached, the Lord began to bless, people began to worship, and then the alarm sounded. I tried to hit the right buttons to reset the alarm only for it to go off a few minutes later. I kept preaching while my wife came up and reset the device every three to five minutes. No one seemed bothered. The Lord continued to bless, and we had a great service. After several weeks, we had the device implanted and were glad for the relief I was getting. We had no idea about the issues we would face years later.

In the meantime, there were other surgeries. I had yet another major surgery on my right ankle and foot. Doctors told me in the days leading up to this surgery that it would be more painful than many of the other previous surgeries. After some four hours of surgery, I awoke in the recovery room with a lot of pain. Surgery on the feet has been some of the more painful surgeries because there is not a lot of tissue in the feet to allow for swelling. Over the next few days, I was given aspirin to help with possible blood clots as well as the usual IV pain medications. After four to five days in the hospital, I was released with the instructions to continue the aspirin and oral pain medications.

We had some of our family in town and my wife left to take them to the usual spots people enjoy seeing when in the central Texas area. Throughout the day, my ears started ringing and I decided to not take the pain medication as often but took two aspirins instead of the one I was told to take. After several hours, I was in a lot of pain and my ears rang even more. Because it had been about three hours since I had last taken the aspirin, I took two more. Within a short time, my ears were ringing even more, and my pain increased by the minute. About two hours later, I decided to take two more aspirins. Within the hour, my ears rang so badly that it was difficult for me to focus or think clearly. I was in major pain by the time my wife arrived home late in the day. I did not want to go to the hospital or call the doctor. I went to bed, thinking it would be better in the morning. By 10 p.m., I was to the point of pulling out my hair from the ringing in my ears and the swelling in my right foot was cutting off the circulation due to the cast being so tight.

One of my wife's few complaints is that I often put off going to the hospital until midnight and disrupt a night's sleep. It was around 11 p.m. when we arrived at the hospital that night. The nurses started an IV but didn't want to give me anything until they knew exactly the cause of the ringing in my ears. Of course, they had my chart from the recent surgery and orders I had been given when discharged from the hospital. I told them what I had done with the aspirin and pain medications throughout the day. The nursing staff contacted the Center for Disease Control (CDC) and reviewed my medication list. The tremendous amount of aspirin contained in the pain medication combined with the what was given in the hospital, the prescription, and the aspirin I had taken, was a recipe for a severe case of ringing ears! They said there was a small chance the ringing could become permanent but should go away in three to four days.

They eventually gave me IV pain medication. Due to the loud ringing, I still felt like I was unable to focus on anything but the ringing. It grew worse and was at a maddening decibel. I also was given medication to help me relax, but it had little affect. The cast on my ankle and foot was turned back into a splint and I was given several large doses of IV pain medication, including valium which should have put me to sleep, but didn't. The pain eased once the cast was loosened, but I was still anxious. Finally, the doctor said there was little more they could do. The best thing was to go home, drink lots of orange juice which would help flush out the aspirin and do what I could to relax. We returned home the next morning as the sun was rising. I felt bad for my wife. I could go to bed, but she had to go to work. When we arrived home, we prayed for God to help me relax and strength for Pamala to make it through the day. I went to the bedroom, put on some gospel music, and tried to focus on the music. My wife decided to lie down before going to work. When I woke up, I was at peace, even though the ringing was still loud. Some may say it was just the medication working, but it had been a long time since they had given me any IV medication. Once again, I began to dwell on how blessed I am and fell asleep thinking about these things.

Chapter 10

FAMILY LIFE

Our boys were now in middle and elementary school. Their friends filled our yard every day after school. Our backyard had a large oak tree where they tied a rope on a limb and did tricks down onto the trampoline. Sometimes, I heard them on the roof and knew they pulled the trampoline against the house to do flips off the roof.

Two memories from that time stand out. On a cold fall morning, my wife got the boys in the car to take them to school. She forgot something and ran back into the house while the boys stayed in the car. Brandon was in the back seat and Chris in the front. I've told them the statute of limitations has run out so they can now be honest, but to this day both boys say they didn't touch anything. Nevertheless, when my wife went back outside, I heard a blood curdling scream. I made my way to the front door and saw our car going backwards in a circle through our driveway, into the street, through our yard, and back into the driveway. The car circled around and around without anyone in it. Brandon jumped out as the car started moving and yelled for Chris to jump as well. When Chris jumped, the back tire ran over his back and legs, grinding his hip into the ground. Since it was cold that morning, the car engine was idling faster than usual. Finally, a man driving to work jumped out of his car and jumped into ours to get it stopped. My wife called my dad to meet her at the hospital. She took Chris to the emergency room in the same car that ran over him. Thankfully, doctors deemed him okay. His side looked like ground beef and he was a bit sore, but his injuries were not serious. My wife framed his clothes with the tire marks visible. God's hand of protection was on my sons that morning. That evening, Chris attended Brandon's baseball practice and earned the nickname "Speed Bump."

Another incident burned in my memory happened while preparing for Wednesday night church. We were in our usual rush when my wife called for us to gather for dinner. Brandon came to the table but there was no sign of Chris. When we couldn't find him, Brandon spoke up and said Chris had taken the car. Chris had previously asked for baseball socks, and I sarcastically said it was impossible to get baseball socks on a Wednesday. I told him that we could get them the next day before his game. "The only way you'll get baseball socks today is if you can drive there yourself," I told him. He took me literally. He grabbed my car keys and headed toward the store. Once he got on a busy four-lane road, just blocks from a major intersection, he realized he had no money. We laugh about that now but when he returned home it was a very serious time. While I scolded him, my wife scolded me.

II Timothy 2:13 says, *"if we believe not, yet he abideth faithful: he cannot deny himself."* As a father, and even more as a grandfather, I can't help myself.

My sons often did things that were wrong, but I can't deny myself. I would have gone after Chris if I had known his whereabouts. I worried about him until he returned. He made a mistake, but I couldn't deny myself. I loved him and wanted him back in my house. The Lord can't deny Himself. He hasn't given us a get-out-of-jail-free card. It isn't an excuse for us to sin, but it is a reason to return to Him when we stumble. He will take us back. He will forgive us, and He knows what we need best at every moment.

Chapter 11

PAIN PUMP

I traveled to Houston to watch Brandon, a high school senior, play in an annual baseball tournament at a high school in The Woodlands. The first night, I returned to my hotel room with extreme nausea. I stayed up all night because I could not control the vomiting. I waited until the next morning to tell my son that I was headed back to Austin. I also called my wife and let her know I was headed back home. The drive should have taken less than three hours, but I kept stopping to vomit. My wife called our family doctor who directed me to come straight to his office. Pamala was waiting for me when I got there. The doctor immediately examined me, realized how sick I was, and sent me across the street to Seton Medical Center to be admitted. I was so dehydrated that it took the nursing staff about 12 attempts before successfully starting an IV. I left the hospital after several days, but eventually landed back in the emergency room. The nausea and uncontrolled vomiting continued. I saw several gastrologists which lead to a referral to the chief of gastroenterology at Baylor Hospital in Dallas. He considered admitting me to the hospital but sent me home after performing a series of tests. We did not get out of Dallas before stopping due to my severe nausea. I was admitted to the hospital again for dehydration after making it back to Austin where doctors decided to send me back to Dallas. This time, the chief of gastroenterology immediately admitted me and performed a lot of tests to determine the cause of the nausea. He got the nausea under control and turned off my pain pump. Once released from the hospital, we started back to Austin and stopped at a restaurant where I got nauseated again. When we arrived back in Austin, physicians removed the pain pump. The nausea slowly subsided over the next few months.

The back pain grew worse when the pain pump was removed, but it was good to no longer deal with constant nausea. I was at the pain management doctor's office talking to the doctor when a representative for a medical device company came along. The representative told us about a trial about to start at a large hospital in Houston. This trial was designed for people who had issues like mine and involved taking synthetic medication. After contacting the trial doctor, I was accepted into the program.

We made the trip to Houston where the doctor informed me that I would need to have another pain pump installed. Thankfully, this medication seemed to work much better than any medication we tried in the past. It not only helped with the pain in my back, but there was no nausea.

During this time, I saw a hematologist for anemia. I needed infusions for my anemia due to my many surgeries and issues. After one of the infusions, I developed a raging headache like I had never experienced before. I ached from head to toe and felt as if I was running a fever. A nurse saw that I was not well and asked if I needed to see the doctor before leaving. I believed I would be okay if I could just get home, take some ibuprofen, and go to bed. By the time I got to my car, I felt like I was coming down with a bad case of the flu or some similar illness. The farther I drove, the worse I felt. My head felt like it was about to explode from the pressure. I had no doubt that I was running a fever.

When I walked into our home, I decided I needed to be rushed to the hospital immediately. I never made that kind of decision on my own. Unplanned trips to the hospital usually only came after begging and pleading from my wife, or after the doctor gave me no other option. I called Pamala to see if she could possibly take me, but she did not answer my call or texts. I later learned that she was in a meeting that required all cell phones be turned off. My sister, Ann, picked me up and drove 90 miles per hour to a small hospital as I moaned in pain the entire way. Ann contacted Pamala and she arrived at the hospital about the time same time we did.

Nurses attempted to start an IV 18 times before calling two anesthesiologists to get the job done. After an MRI, I was transported to the larger Seton hospital, about a 10-minute ambulance ride away. There I was put in ICU and connected to many machines and IV bags of medication. Dr. Jack Bissett, an infectious disease doctor who previously treated me for several serious infections, diagnosed me with spinal meningitis. The catheter leading to my spinal cord and connected to the pain pump became infected. The pain pump and catheter needed to be removed.

Chapter 12

TOUCHING HEAVEN

When it came time for my surgery, Pamala called The Pentecostals of Alexandria and asked for Sis. Vesta Mangun or Bro. Anthony Mangun. The Manguns had been a great support to my family during a difficult spiritual challenge and had become close to my family. My sons loved Bro. G.A. and Sis. Vesta and considered them spiritual grandparents. Bro. Anthony and Sis. Mickey Mangun called us and prayed for us during several serious medical challenges. When our boys were in high school, we went out of our way to Alexandria at the end of summer vacation so our boys could be around the Mangun family and the church. These spiritual giants would always take time to encourage our sons and lift our spirits.

My wife told Sis. Vesta about our desperate situation as nurses wheeled me into the operating room. Sis. Vesta asked to be put on speaker phone so she could pray for both of us at the same time. Pamala walked beside the stretcher holding the cell phone while Sis. Vesta prayed, spoke in tongues, and commanded healing in the name of Jesus. Anyone nearby could hear. As the nurses walked into the operating room, my wife continued walking alongside the stretcher while Sis. Vesta loudly and boldly asked for God to intervene in the situation. The nursing staff tried to stop my wife but there was no stopping her.

Everyone in the operating room listened to this woman on speaker phone binding the enemy, praying for the doctors, and claiming healing. Someone asked who was on the phone and why my wife was allowed into the operating room. The doctor said it was important that the surgery get under way immediately, but my wife told him the phone call was far more important than anything else that could take place. Pamala told the doctor that a very important person was on the phone, and she couldn't hang up.

When Sis. Mangun stopped praying, my wife kissed me, and walked out of the operating room. For the first time that day, I was at peace, though still in pain from meningitis. I'm thankful for those who are instant in prayer. There is not a long runway of prayer needed for them to begin to pray in the spirit. These are people who stay in prayer and are ready to do spiritual battle at any time. To be able to step into a spirit of prayer instantly takes staying in a mode of constant and faithful prayer.

My mom is another person who can instantly move into a place of touching heaven without needing to prepare her heart first. I've seen those who are too stoic to pray in church. They can't worship because "it isn't their personality" to be vocal in prayer and praise. However, those same people have no problem being vocal in their prayer when something happens in their family or when a loved one goes into ICU!

> We never know what tomorrow holds. We never know what might happen between the time we walk out of one service and the next. Having a daily walk with God and building a prayer life that keeps the communication open with God is of the utmost importance. I don't necessarily spend two to three-hour blocks of time a day

in prayer, but I do take time throughout the day to stop and pray for 30 minutes or so. I can move into prayer quickly if I first listen to Gospel music or a sermon and then read a few verses from the Bible. I begin with praise. I tell God how great He is and thank Him for what He has done in my life. Like King David, I always repent. I want my heart clean of things I am unaware are in me. After repentance, I present my needs to Him.

On many occasions, Pamala and I have sat in the hospital or at a doctor's office and asked God to move in our situation. I don't understand how people cope with life without taking their needs to God. It is so wonderful to be able to hand Him the burden and weight of the worry and concern we are experiencing!

I remained in the hospital for approximately three weeks with meningitis. The first few days were very painful, and I was in ICU for the first week. When I was moved to a regular hospital room, a hospital internist saw a book on prayer next to my bed. He asked if I believed in prayer. I shared a very abbreviated bit of my testimony with him of how God spared my life and healed me time and time again. He asked me to pray for a need in his family that only prayer could resolve.

We are in a world that is troubled on all sides. There are those who believe in prayer, but they are not sure God hears their prayer. I believe when we are bold enough to go beyond just saying, "I'll keep you in my prayers" and actually pray for them in the moment, we can enable their faith. Pamala and I have prayed for people at the grocery store, hospital, and other businesses. We usually stop and ask if they mind us praying for them, then in a quiet way we pray God will answer their prayer request, bring them peace of mind, rest at night, and that they feel God leading them through whatever it is they are facing. I feel by praying for them on the spot and making physical contact with them by touching their arm for example, we are helping convince them God does hear their prayer. On many occasions, we've had people contact us and let us know from that point God began working in their lives. Titus 2:13 speaks of "the blessed hope." Believers can be conduits to help others experience that blessed hope that only comes from Jesus Christ.

Chapter 13

$1,500 MIRACLE

The nurses struggled to start IVs each time we came in the hospital. Often my veins would blow just after a day, and they would have to start over in another spot. The decision was made to install a central venous catheter, a central line which goes all the way up to a vein near the heart. It is used in place of a regular IV line because it can stay in up to a year and makes giving medication and drawing blood much easier. Patients can also be given much larger amounts of medication or fluids. The central line allowed me to go home from the hospital after recovering from meningitis and receive IV antibiotics at home.

Receiving the IV at home was a $1,500 miracle! I really didn't want to go into a rehabilitation center, but the $1,500 cost was too much. We did what we learned to do. We prayed. Pamala spoke with the patient advocate, begging for a way we could go home on the IV antibiotics. Seton Medical Center is a Catholic hospital and the Daughters of Charity are a big part of it. A nun known simply as Sis. B was over the Daughters of Charity. She was known for standing up to the medical staff, doctors, and administrators for a cause in which she believed. We were given a day to make our decision. We didn't have $1500 to give to the hospital, but I was determined I was NOT going to a rehab center. All we knew to do was pray one more time. The next day, Sis. B walked into my hospital room and said, "I heard you had a big need." I told her we were deciding between a rehabilitation center or finding a way to pay for the antibiotics. Sis. B said, "I have something for you." She laid an envelope on the hospital tray. It contained a check for $1500. Anyone who tries to tell me prayer doesn't work is wasting their time. I am a firm believer in prayer.

In John 11, Jesus was told his friend, Lazarus, was sick. In verse 4, Jesus says very emphatically, that the sickness was not unto death, but for the glory of God. Lazarus had been dead for four days by the time Jesus arrived at his tomb. On His way, Jesus told His disciples that Lazarus was sleeping. They thought it was good for the sick man to get much needed rest. Jesus had to tell them straight out that Lazarus was not sleeping but dead. Thomas said, "let us go and die with him." His faith was completely gone. The disciples told Jesus the Jews were lying in wait to stone him so he should stay away from his sick friend.

In several instances, Jesus simply spoke and people in need received their healing. In Matthew 8, a Roman centurion came to Jesus and said his servant was lying at home paralyzed and very sick. When Jesus offered to go to his home, the centurion said, "Speak the word. I am a man of authority and I tell the soldiers to go and they go. I tell them to do this and they do it." Jesus told the Roman centurion he could go home because due to his faith, his servant was healed. Jesus took a 12-year-old girl by the hand and raised her from the dead. A widow woman's son had died. In the middle of his funeral procession, Jesus raised him by the hand.

Jesus could have just as easily spoken the healing of Lazarus the instant he heard Lazarus was ill. At any point over the following days, Jesus could have spoken and immediately Lazarus would have been healed. Jesus, as God manifest in flesh, knew when Lazarus died. As Mary and Martha prepared his body for burial, Jesus could have given the word and Lazarus would have been raised from the dead instantly! The friends of Lazarus would have seen or heard of his healing or being raised from the dead but that was not the will of God.

There are times we pray and want God to do an instant work. Some of our greatest questions come when it seems as if Jesus is not hearing our prayer and we don't receive that instant answer. We know God can immediately change the circumstances we face. We pray, we believe, and we may even fast and have others praying and fasting on our behalf. We wonder why God delays doing the work we know He can do in our lives.

The miracle of Lazarus is the seventh miracle in the gospel of John. John wrote about fewer miracles than are found in the other gospels. Each of the miracles that John lists are a sign of what God is going to do in the church. The church was birthed on the day of Pentecost and John wants to show what God will do in His church. The first miracle is the turning of water into wine, resulting in the best wine served last. Christ is saving his best days for the last days. The seventh miracle John tells is this story of Lazarus who had two sisters, Mary and Martha. Jesus stayed at their home on many occasions. Their home was a place for Jesus to minister at times. The Bible makes it clear that Jesus was a friend of Lazarus. Jesus wanted to prove to the world there was no doubt that He was the son of God. He was God in flesh. It is amazing to consider no one ever died in the presence of Jesus. Jesus wouldn't be with them much longer. He desired to remove all doubt about who He was and the authority He had. There were skeptics and critics who tried to disprove the miracles of Jesus. He wanted to prove to them, once and for all, who He was, that He could heal the sick, and He could take authority over death itself.

Jesus referred to Lazarus as "sleeping" because death in this life isn't the end for the child of God. In this seventh miracle told in John's gospel, Jesus was told that Lazarus was not only dead and buried in a tomb but had been dead for so long he was decaying and started to stink! Jesus wanted them to know death wasn't going to have the final say. What good would it have been had Jesus opened the blinded eye, unstopped the deaf ear, and healed those with leprosy, but couldn't raise the dead?

The Bible refers to death as the last enemy. Jesus Christ not only overcame all sicknesses but death, hell, and the grave! Death was not the ultimate ruler of Lazarus and is not the ultimate ruler over you, or me! When told of Lazarus' death, Jesus replied, "I'm glad," because He wanted to use the death of Lazarus to show the glory of God.

I don't receive an immediate answer for every trial because there are times God wants to use us to show forth His glory through us to those around us. My walk with God is not just about God blessing me or instantly answering every prayer when I'm in need. Each time I face a difficult challenge in my life, I know people are watching my life and they will see the glory of God in the way I come through those times of great need. I'm thankful for every time God instantly answers my prayer, but I'm also thankful for every time He carries me through trials while others see the grace and mercy of God in my situation.

God blessing me is not about me. God always abundantly blesses those used for His glory. Job was blessed and given far more than he ever had. The woman with the oil was used by God and filled not only her pots, but the pots of all her neighbors. When we go through a trial, it is more than just about us. It is for the glory of God. Our lives can bring glory to God.

You may feel you've written the final chapter of your life, that you've put the pen down, and there is no hope. The Bible says God can make all things new. There is hope! God can take what you think is the end, bring hope and healing, and make you into a testimony for all those around you to see His glory.

Lazarus was in the tomb, tightly bound by grave clothes. I'm not sure he could have risen and walked if he wanted to do so. I believe the spirit of God picked him up and moved him to the front of the tomb. Those around Jesus were told to remove the stone and Jesus simply said, "Lazarus, come forth." They were then told to remove the grave clothes of Lazarus and unbind his feet and hands. God is not looking at your situation as the end. You could spend hours asking God why you can't see what you want to see in your life. He simply says, "Give it to me. This is not the end!"

When Jesus spoke the word for Lazarus to come back to life, He could have also just spoken the word and the stone would have crumbled at His command, but their rolling the stone away was an act of faith. When they did all they could, Jesus then did His part. God knows the situations we face are not the end. No problem is too great for Him. The greater the problem, the more glory He receives. He wants us to do our part, which is prayer, fasting, reading His Word, and being faithful to Him. When we have done our part, He will always step in and do His part. Jesus wants us unbound. He desires that we be freed from anything that would bind us so that we can bring Him glory. He wants our hands free so we can worship Him and our feet free so we can go tell others about what He has done in our lives. If we will establish daily disciplines in our life, even death itself is not the end. If we can get to know Him by developing a consistent daily walk with Him, then He will bring life to any situation we face.

There is hope for your children. They can live for God.

There is hope for your health. The doctor's report is not the final say.

There is hope for your finances. The bank account printout isn't the final word.

Jesus Christ can, and will, bring life to whatever the enemy has stolen from you. Jesus wants all of you. He wants more than a Sunday and maybe a Wednesday night Bible study. If you will give Him every part of your life, Jesus Christ can speak to your situation, even if it seems that things have started to decay, and you are long past all hope. Hold onto the hand of God in the midst of trouble.

I pray those things in your life that you feel are dead will come back to life as Jesus Christ speaks to your situation. You have not written the final chapter no matter your current situation. You are about to be delivered and bring glory to God!

Chapter 14

SEPTIC!

The central line was ready to be replaced almost a year later. My wife was working. Since this was going to be a short procedure, I asked my dad to go with me. The surgeon explained this procedure would take just a few minutes and I would be at the hospital for just a few hours, so I wasn't concerned. My dad stayed with me until they took me back to get prepared for the surgery. It was close to lunch time, so I told him to go eat lunch at a nearby restaurant. By the time he returned, I would be close to being ready for the return home. I put on the hospital gown, the socks and head covering. I climbed onto the gurney and let the nurse know I was ready. She came in and took my vitals and went over the usual paperwork. She made the usual small talk as she took the vitals and discussed past procedures. After about 15 minutes, she came back and said she wanted to recheck my vitals. This time, she seemed more serious and was paying close attention to each of the vital signs. She looked at the thermometer a bit longer and double checked my blood pressure and pulse. She said the surgeon was finishing up with the patient before me and would be out shortly. Another 30 minutes passed and the same nurse came out and said she wanted to recheck my temperature because it was a little under 100 degrees. The surgeon said he wouldn't go through with replacing the line if I had a temperature. I had a fever of 99.5 degrees, so the procedure was canceled.

I pleaded my case. I didn't feel bad. My temperature was not even 100 degrees. I took time to come there for the surgery. I didn't understand why he wasn't going forward with the procedure. The surgeon admitted me to the hospital for blood work and observation.

It wasn't long before my dad returned to the hospital, fully expecting to pick me up to take me home. I was upset and fussed at the doctor and nursing staff. Why would I be admitted to the hospital when my temperature registered less than a full degree below 100? The transport staff arrived and moved me from the pre-surgical area to a hospital room. I apologized to my dad for wasting his time and was upset with the doctor for wasting mine. The nursing staff tried to reason with me as they drew blood. If nothing showed in the bloodwork and my temperature was normal overnight, the central line would be replaced the next morning. It was worth the 24-hour delay if I had an infection of some kind. My dad tried to tell me it wasn't a waste of his time. I called Pamala and she had told me it was no big deal, and everything would be fine.

I felt feverish a little over an hour after I arrived in the hospital room. I began shaking with chills and my teeth chattered. I felt so cold! By now, the nurses were taking my temperature every 15 minutes or so. My temperature rose to over 104 degrees. I went from freezing to burning up, hot with fever, and feeling extremely sick. Pamala arrived at the hospital not long after my temperature rose above 104. Before she got to my room, a male nurse who was close to retirement and had been my nurse on many occasions, told my wife that I was septic. The line and my blood became infected. The doctor gave me a 50/50 chance of surviving the infection.

When they brought dinner to the floor that evening, the smell of food caused me to get nauseated to the point I began to throw up. I went without eating for days. I couldn't even drink anything without getting nauseated. Each time the food trays were brought to the floor, the staff or my wife would close the door to my room. The dietitian did everything to find something I could keep down, to no avail. I was offered soups, broth, and protein drinks, but I couldn't put anything close to my mouth without getting sick. I went so long without food my breath began to stink. The dietitian said this happened when going long periods without any food or water.

After two full weeks of intravenous antibiotics and little improvement with the infection and nausea, the infectious disease doctor said he tried about every combination of antibiotics and wasn't making any headway with the infection. He fought trying to find the right combination of antibiotics to overcome the infections and finding medications to combat the severe nausea. He asked, "why is it with you it always seem so complicated?" I had no answer. I often asked myself and God that question. Why couldn't I just have surgery without there being some accompanying issues? For three weeks, I couldn't think about eating. For three weeks, it was difficult to drink water, juice, or broth of any flavor because just the smell of food would cause me to begin vomiting. It wasn't just throwing up, but it was a violent nausea that hurt my back. I tried to eat children's popsicles containing Pedialyte, but that didn't work. We tried anything that would give me some sort of nutrition. The nursing staff would pour a cup of water and come in every 15 minutes to see if I got some measured portion down. Nothing seemed to work. I would take a small sip and couldn't force myself to drink anymore. I was weak. My fever would break for a few hours only to return.

The hospital internist reviewed with me some of the serious health issues I had faced over the previous few years. He said what I was currently facing was so serious there was a chance I may not leave the hospital alive. He suggested I write a letter to my sons telling them how much I loved them and cared for them. If I didn't survive, I would have something in writing that they could read later and know I was proud of them and sorry I could not be there to watch them grow up, attend their weddings, and spend time with any future grandchildren. This stunned me. I knew I was in a serious condition, but this brought everything into focus. I got out my laptop and thought I would type a letter to each of my boys. I was weak in body and my mind wasn't all that clear. I stared at my computer screen for several hours. I would write something only to erase it because everything I wrote sounded so petty. I thought having a pen and paper would be easier, so I got a legal pad out of my backpack and sat staring at a blank page. I would write something but tear up the page and toss it in the trash because it sounded trite. What do you tell your sons that will make a lasting impact and will be meaningful to their lives 20 years later?

Finally, I gave up trying to come up with the perfect words or writing something that was profoundly wise. I simply put on paper that words would never come close to telling them how proud I was of them and how much I loved them. Only when they had children of their own would they realize the love of a parent for a child. I wrote that I was sorry I didn't live to see them grow up but they had a great mom and she would see to it that they grew up to be wonderful young men. I told them to take care of their mother and respect her because they were already young men and would need to take on additional responsibility. The only advice I could offer was to serve God with your all their heart, soul, and mind because nothing in this life was of greater importance than living for God. If they gave God every area of their lives, God would enable them to be the best men they could be and we would be able to join together in the land that is eternal and has no death or sorrow. Tears streamed down my face as I wrote these two letters. I took almost six hours to write two very short but simple letters. I held onto them. Thankfully, I didn't have to give them the letters because God brought me out of the hospital. Nevertheless, that remains one of the harder things I have done.

Instead of reading the letters, I began telling them what I wanted to convey in those letters. When I arrived home, I went in their rooms after they fell asleep and prayed for God to watch over them and allow them to grow up into men who lived faithful lives for God. I continued the routine until they both left for college. Because of my continual pain, I woke up several times throughout the night. Instead of just lying in bed, I went into my sons' bedrooms and prayed that God's hand would be on them the following day, that He would continually draw them to Him, and that God would convict them when they were tempted. There were nights I felt God's presence strong, and my prayer became more earnest and vocal. On several occasions, one of my sons would wake up and say, "Dad, we can't sleep because you are praying too loudly." I had been at a point of writing letters to my sons because I was so close to death. I felt

God brought me through and allowed me to live. I wasn't going to waste this opportunity to fight for them spiritually.

Early on after my accident, people said things to me which were out of line. People told me God wasn't healing me because I had some sin or desire God wanted me to give up. I agree that God has ways of getting our attention, and when we go through a trial, we should examine our lives to make sure there is nothing God would love for us to lay down. However, I had repented and repented again. I moved closer to God in my walk. I was far from perfect, but I did everything I could to serve God.

While in the hospital room very sick from the infection, people came by my room to say maybe God wanted me to give up something, repent of something, tell someone I was sorry about something, or some other thing that would allow God to heal me. Job faced his friends saying much the same thing. One person told me that God would instantly heal me if I would just give everything to Him and repent of whatever I was hiding in my heart. Since this person wore glasses and a hearing aide, I asked if he had considered that maybe God would heal his eyesight and hearing if he would repent. This person looked at me somewhat stunned and walked away, never again suggesting to me I needed to repent.

I'm glad God will slow me down at times and let me know there are things I need to give to Him. That said, not every trial is because I've done something against God. Sometimes, it is just life. Other times, it may be to bring Him glory. I never want to get sick and not search my heart or check to make sure God isn't trying to tell me something.

In Hebrews 11, the heroes of faith faced horrible trials. Those names are in Hebrews precisely because of what they faced, with some dying horrible deaths. It was not because they lacked faith. They are heroes of faith. It wasn't because they were sinful or were far from God. If you go through a trial, check your life, but don't let

Satan convince you God doesn't love you.

The story of Peter denying the Lord three times in one night, after being warned by God, is a tale of caution. When the Lord rose from the grave, one of the first things he asked was, "Where is Peter?" I'm glad we serve a merciful God. I'm glad we serve a God who will take us back. In the middle of a great trial, the enemy of my soul loves to convince me God doesn't care for me because maybe I have sinned. Nobody knows our scars, wounds, or the times we've stubbed our toe as well as we do; yet, when I'm in need, God is like the father of the prodigal who meets us when we return to Him.

After over three weeks of not eating and barely getting down any liquid, Pamala and I prayed for God to give me healing and to give doctors the answers they sought. We reached a point of desperation. The infection presented an extremely serious problem, and the nausea presented another serious challenge. The doctors and I were concerned we would soon have little choice but to move forward with a feeding tube.

Pamala attended church that Sunday morning and took communion. She brought the communion elements from service to the hospital. She took out the bread and the juice and the two of us prayed once again for God to hear our desperate cry and give us the answers we so desperately needed. As an ordinary husband and wife, we took communion. There were no earthquakes, no audible voice from the heavens, and I wasn't instantly and miraculously touched. In fact, I didn't feel much of anything out of the ordinary. Taking communion is always moving as we search our hearts.

Communion is following the instructions of Jesus Christ, who said, "do this in remembrance of me." We take the juice which represents the blood of Christ that was shed for us. The bread represents His broken body for our sins. I wanted that special anointing of the Lord to sweep in, hoping we would feel the supernatural break the chains that had bound us for weeks. At least the juice and bread stayed down and didn't come back up! I didn't feel a reassurance that God had taken note. There wasn't anything memorable I can pinpoint when I felt God intervene and give us a reassurance that I would walk out of the hospital. Pamala had rushed straight from church, not even stopping to get something for her lunch. She didn't let on that she was disappointed the miraculous didn't immediately occur, but she had faith that God was going to make everything all right. I wasn't instantly healed, but rested better that afternoon than I had in some time.

The next morning, I woke up with an overwhelming hunger for Chicago-style, deep dish pizza from a certain pizza place in Austin. I begged for it until she gave in, drove to the place, and bought a pizza. When she came back, she cut a small piece off a slice. I begged for more. Because I hadn't eaten anything for three weeks, she was afraid I would get sick. The nurse told me to take it easy, to eat some broth or soup first. But I was craving that deep dish pizza to the point I wanted to lick the sauce off the inside of the box! Slowly, Pamala fed me one small bite at a time, waiting for a long while between each bite. I ate the remainder of the pizza over the next two days. When Pamala was at work, I ordered a pizza to be delivered from that same pizza restaurant. That day, I had no one to stop me and I ate the whole pizza until I was nauseated from overeating!

The doctors prepared us for the possibility that I may not survive the infection. I had been extremely ill, but God moved on the scene one more time and spared my life. I can't explain the "why" and I can't tell you how God healed me, but I can tell you I would not be here if God wasn't the Healer of all diseases. The name of Jesus can heal all disease. The name of Jesus can bring peace to every home, mend the most broken relationships, bring hope to your finances, and calm every storm.

Chapter 15

WEIGHT GAIN – HEALTHY LIFESTYLE

It is easy to feel like your life is over when you suffer from chronic pain. You tend to just exist. A major disease or accident will cause many to feel as if their best days are in the past. The pain or disease can too often become a crutch used as an excuse to stay at home and not get out. I was in great physical condition before the accident. I lifted weights, ran almost daily, and enjoyed playing many different sports. Working out and jogging had been my favorite methods of relaxing since the age of 13 or 14 up until October 18, 1982. Until my accident, I never considered watching my diet. My dad was overweight, and I spent many days encouraging him to join me in exercising. Now, I had gained almost 100 pounds and was more overweight than my dad! I used my chronic pain as an excuse for not exercising and getting in shape.

My dad worked closely with my wife from the day of my accident to help take care of my needs. He helped change bandages and do wound care. He took me to the doctor or hospital when my wife was unable. He paid for prescriptions when money was tight for us. He did whatever we needed. He was very close to my sons and his other grandchildren and spent a lot of time with them. His weight led to a series of strokes which resulted in several serious medical issues, and ultimately admission to a long- term care facility. My dad passed away in his early 70s in July 2011.

Shortly after my dad's death, Brandon and his wife announced they were having their first child and our first grandchild. My sedentary lifestyle and unhealthy diet translated to high blood pressure and other health issues not directly related to my accident. When I learned I was going to be a grandfather, I made up my mind I wasn't going to be like my dad and die in my early 70s. I vowed my chronic pain would no longer stop me from the things I enjoyed.

Pamala asked me on many occasions to join her on an afternoon walk. I used all the foot, knee, hip, and back pain as an excuse to halt everything I enjoyed. One day, I finally agreed to go with her. We walked at most one-tenth mile and I was in major pain. My feet hurt and my back ached so badly I felt as if I was going to pass out from the pain. I barely made it back to the house. Something inside of me welled up and I grew angry. I allowed myself to get so out of shape. I realized if I didn't make up my mind, I would be in a similar condition as my father. I decided to stop using chronic pain as an excuse and start living. I couldn't jog. I would never work out like I once had, but I would do as much as I could today and would do more tomorrow.

My neighbor inspired me to do more. In his 80s, he competed in marathons across the United States.

Surely, I could get to the place where I could walk at least one mile per day. I promised Pamala we would walk the next day and set our goal for the large oak tree about 200 yards beyond where we walked the first day. We reached our goal and a little beyond the next afternoon. We extended our goal a little farther each day. The summers are hot and muggy in central Texas, but that didn't deter us. A few weeks later, I began changing my diet. I knew a fad diet wouldn't work. I had to change my lifestyle. I gave up soft drinks. Instead of fried foods I ate blackened or grilled foods. I cut out bread and sweets and made a few other simple changes. It was difficult at first. To keep me on track, I bought a scale and weighed myself the first thing every morning. I didn't lose any weight for the first two weeks. When I finally saw the scale numbers gradually decrease, I felt proud of my accomplishment. By the time my grandson was born eight months later, I had lost 50 pounds, I lost a total of 100 over about a two-year period. We walked on the cold and hot days. If the weather was bad enough to prevent us from walking, we walked in a nearby mall. The back pain which had been excruciating when I first started walking gradually disappeared. The knee pain remained until I had one knee replaced for the second time. My knees had already been replaced in 2010 and 2011, but the pain had worsened.

Walking and diet changes brought physical and mental improvement. My blood pressure returned to normal, and I was taken off all blood pressure medication. Every one of my doctors, including my dentist, saw vast improvements in my health. I'm impatient, but I realized it had taken decades to gain the weight. I realized in my 50s the weight would take time to lose. My goal was never to lose 100 pounds. My goal was to walk and eat a healthy diet each day. I slept better at night. My mental outlook improved because I was active in ways I hadn't been in years. After two years of walking each day, Pamala and I walked upwards of five miles a day. I walked as far as eight to 10 miles on several occasions just to see how far I could push myself! Our first grandson, Gentry, was born on February 1, 2016, our second grandson, Levi, was born April 25, 2017, and our third grandchild was a girl, Olivia, born on August 20, 2018. Between my dad's death and the birth of my grandchildren, I had the incentive to lose weight and get as healthy as possible.

I stopped driving around parking lots looking for the nearest spot to the front door of the building. Instead, I parked away from the door so I would walk farther. I looked for reasons to add to my daily steps. Because I was in better shape, I did things with my family I otherwise couldn't have done. I enjoyed traveling because I could walk and see the sites. I took my grandchildren to theme parks to ride roller coasters, taught my grandsons to swim, and rediscovered things I had not been able to enjoy for several years. I blamed everything on my accident when really it was because I didn't stay healthy. I had many physical limitations, but because I pushed myself, I regained a greater quality of life.

Starting from square one again is difficult. I found if I set a goal of both starting over and a goal of how far I will walk each week, I am more likely to begin anew. There is no doubt in my mind that God can do the miraculous and instant work of physical healing. God has healed me and my wife instantly in the past. I also believe God wants me to do my part in staying healthy. If I pray for God to heal me and continue doing the exercises after formal physical therapy is finished, God can work through those exercises and help me overcome the physical limitations I may experience.

For those who have long-term chronic pain, it can be easy to gain weight or feel captive to a disease or event that happened in your life. I have been told by counselors, physicians, and physical therapists that people will either fight or give into the pain. Those who give into the pain will find themselves trapped by the pain. Some surgeons have stopped performing physical therapy after surgeries for things like artificial knee replacement because patients refuse to do their exercises at home. Six to eight weeks of physical therapy is useless if patients don't continue to move after the surgery. They will end up in the same conditions as they were pre-surgery.

I prayed and asked God for strength and will power to push myself, I see the difference it makes when I eat healthy and walk daily. I feel better mentally and physically. I allow myself a cheat day at times. Sometimes, I reward myself for eating healthy and walking daily by eating something sweet or a couple of pieces of fried chicken. I enjoy date nights with my wife and eating a good meal followed by sharing a dessert. Often, we have people visit us at our home and I will eat a small piece of dessert with our guests. Overall, however, the joy of losing weight, feeling healthy, and exercising daily is enough to keep me on track.

I have bought all types of workout machines, but used them for just a few weeks, then they would sit idle until we finally sold them. I have joined several local gyms in hopes of working out consistently, but for me, there is nothing as relaxing as walking with my wife. We don't walk the same route every day. Walking daily gives us time together and helps us physically. There are several wooded areas around our home and walking through the woods while the birds are chirping is very relaxing. We've even carried a picnic lunch with us, stopped to eat, and listened to the wind in the trees and the local wildlife nearby. We use apps to keep track of how far we walk. I am forced to go slower than most, but in about an hour we can cover three miles. Our normal walk ranges from an hour to 90 minutes depending on what time of year it is and what we have going on that day. Science has developed many wonderful new aids for those in chronic pain, but I don't know of anything that is as helpful as getting outside, soaking up the sun and vitamin D, and exploring the world around us. It may be a nearby subdivision, a nearby park, or a wooded area. If you have physical challenges or long-term chronic pain, try going outside to soak up the sun and explore.

A new subdivision was under construction near us, and we walked across the cleared land every evening. One day, a salesman came out of the model home and said he had seen us walk by daily and offered us the use of his restroom or a bottle of water anytime we wished. He said our commitment to walking impressed him and he wanted to meet us. From that time, we stopped and visited him and then invited him to church. When we get out, God can open doors to share our testimony with those around us. That opportunity would have never presented itself if we had we been inside on a treadmill.

My accident caused a prominent limp, obvious scars, and other physical issues. Small children stare and point at me at times. Even my own grandsons give me a hard time about how I walk. One day, while I was throwing a baseball with them, they told me I had to be the slowest runner to have ever lived! But I can walk! Had I not lost weight, I would not be able to play baseball or soccer with them. Instead, I would have been indoors feeling sorry for myself. There was a time when I was told I may never walk. I'm alive and it is up to me to choose what to do with what

God has given me. I chose to get out and enjoy life. The more weight I lost, the better I felt about myself and the more confident I became.

I can't jog anymore, but most of the orthopedic doctors said the stress on the knees, feet and hips are much less when walking than jogging. At times, I walk so slowly that my wife gets ahead and is forced to wait on me. If I can walk three miles each day after three knee replacements and four hip replacements, you can do it as well. This achievement takes time and patience. This must be done one day at a time with determination to get back on track if you fall off the wagon. I knew I wasn't disciplined enough to stick to any of the well-known diet programs for the long term, but I could cut out soft drinks, bread, fried foods, and desserts. I never felt starved. I ate fruits for snacks instead of sweets. Eating at a slower pace rather than gulping down my food also helped. If you are a chronic pain patient, I encourage you to start a program that gets you outside and moving. There are lots of options, whether it's going to the YMCA or walking at a local mall. I've been told by doctors when we walk, the joints tell the brain to send fluid to your joints which makes you feel less stiff. Many people asked me how I lost weight. I saw the disappointment in their faces when I told them I had made a change in my diet and walked daily. They wanted something quick and easy. They sought some secret that would make quick changes and allow them to lose weight while eating what they wanted.

I made myself eat breakfast every morning. I ate something nutritious for lunch, and a healthy, but filling meal, for dinner. I packed my lunch if I was going to be out and about, instead of going to a fast- food restaurant.

An injury, chronic pain, or disease doesn't have to be the end of a fulfilling life. Consult your family doctor and have them suggest an activity you can do which will not cause harm, as well as offer a diet plan to aid you in losing any weight you may have gained. My weight loss meant I got off high blood pressure medication and was in less pain when I walked. The mental part of losing weight and performing a physical activity is worth any sacrifice you may have to make. John 14:14 tells us that, "If ye ask anything in my name, I will do it" (KJV). I believe that includes asking God to help us maintain a healthy diet and He will enable us to exercise so that we improve our health.

By 2014, I had both knees replaced. In fact, the left knee had been replaced twice and now the doctors said hip replacement could no longer be delayed. The knee replacements were some of the less painful surgeries I have experienced. My knees got to the point that doctors drained them monthly. Between swelling from fluid build-up and the bone-on-bone pain, walking was difficult. My left knee swelled when I started my daily walks with my wife. We were walking up to four miles a day when the swelling increased, and the pain became difficult to bear. The bone-on-bone pain greatly limited the distance I walked each day. Dr. Smoot gave me several steroid injections. When that no longer worked, he injected a product known as Synvisc, which acts as a replacement of your natural knee fluid. It stopped working after a while, so Dr. Smoot scheduled a knee replacement. I was expected to do well with the replacement surgery since I had been walking daily. The second day after surgery, a machine was placed on my knee to bend and stretch it. I got impatient after several days of using the machine at home. I decided to set a timer and increase how far back the machine bent my knee every hour. It was painful, but by the end of the day, I had more range of motion than expected. When I contacted the home health agency and told them I was finished with the machine, they were shocked. I could flex my newly replaced knee more than the knee which hadn't been replaced! I worked on strengthening my knee and stretching out the parts that had not been stretched for a long time. I went to physical therapy for only about three weeks and reached all the goals the therapists set.

The second knee replacement came six months later. This time, the machine to stretch and bend my knee was no longer used by Dr. Smoot. I did about two weeks physical therapy and was released. In just a few weeks, I resumed my daily walks, logging three miles without pain or swelling.

Sadly, the therapist who worked with me after many surgeries began to struggle to do simple tasks. Ashley was in her early 30s, had played on the University of Texas soccer team, and had recently married. She began to do what some refer to as table surfing, using a table as support to walk and only letting loose of it to grab hold of another. Ashley once walked with a bounce and was full of energy. I watched a man in his mid-30s complain about exercising on a total gym. Ashley jumped on the total gym, stood it upright, placed her hands on the foot pedal, and did 10 handstands in just a few seconds. Ashley always laughed and joked with those around her. She helped me through severe pain after several major surgeries and got me back on my feet. Now, she struggled to stand and grew weaker and weaker. Doctors eventually diagnosed her with a brain tumor and performed surgery to remove it. Her surgery appeared to be successful at first, but her tumor returned. She died a few months later. I remember the first time I walked into physical therapy and asked why Ashley wasn't there. I knew the answer as the other therapists looked around at each other without saying anything. Finally, one of the therapists, with tears in her eyes, said Ashely passed away two days prior. She died between my appointments. My mind went back to those times when she asked me how I could go on after facing one test after another. It opened the door for me to tell her how God had given me strength and peace of mind in the worst of times.

We never know whom our lives will touch or to whom our struggles will provide strength when facing great difficulty. Ashley helped me through painful times in physical therapy. She said my story of overcoming by God's grace and mercy compelled her to lean on God as she faced brain cancer. She said stories about how God held us tighter as my wife and I clung tighter to God sustained her. Ashley found herself praying for God to do the same for her. She had not prayed since she was a young girl but started praying daily for God to give her rest at night and strength in the daytime.

I have many more questions than answers as to why we face issues in this life. I do know it is a wonderful feeling to help someone dealing with a terminal disease. I could not have helped her had I not faced health issues. People watch how we respond to crisis situations. We can show them how God brings us through great trials that try our faith. If we can get through times of great heartache and pain with the peace of God in our hearts, we can touch the lives of those around us, even with those we may never hear our testimony. There are many Ashleys around us each day. They may never share their struggles or the upheaval in their lives, but by watching us as

Christians, they can see we have a peace that goes beyond all understanding. They know we can walk through the very shadow of the valley of death and not fear. I want to be a positive influence on those around me. I don't want to drag them down. We can put them in touch with a God who loves them and will pour His mercy out on their lives, but we must live the life of an overcomer even when we are in the middle of a trial.

Chapter 16

AGAIN?

I reached a point where I could no longer delay my hip replacement. The pain became too severe, I could not sleep at night, and was unable to perform my daily walk without a lot of pain. My greatest pain came at night when lying down. It worsened with time. Dr. Smoot suggested I see a young doctor who specialized in hip surgery. When I met Dr. Logan, I found him to have the same demeanor of many of those at that orthopedic group. He was personal, caring, and came with a pedigree. He ordered an MRI of my hip which showed there was no cartilage left. There was little to do but replace my hip. However, while examining my hip, he said I would need to visit Dr. Smoot about my left knee which seemed to be far too loose. A few days later, Dr. Smoot examined my knee and then ordered an MRI to get a better look at what caused the knee to be so loose. The plastic portions of the artificial knee had worn at a bad angle due to how I walked. Dr. Smoot said I needed to undergo another knee replacement before having the hip replacement. I was discouraged.

There are times I've gone to the condominium where I fell and said, "Okay, God, how much is enough?" I wanted to get the hip replacement behind me and move forward but had to go through the process of having a knee replacement first. Though the knees hadn't been a difficult surgery, the process of getting the knee to the place I could have the hip surgery was more than I was ready to face. I've gotten good at getting my mind right for surgery. I start several weeks out, if possible, and start to pump myself up as if it is a sporting event. I get in my laser-focused mindset and prepare to face the challenge.

I had the knee surgery and God brought us through in record time. He knew I needed all my strength and courage to go through my hip surgery. In just a few weeks, I was walking every day, although my hip became quite painful. To see how far I could walk with my new knee, I walked 10 miles two days before my hip replacement surgery.

In the summer of 2015, just a few months after my knee replacement, Dr. Smoot cleared me for hip surgery. Wearing any medical device can be tiresome, but it can get unbearable in the 100+ degree Texas summer heat. If possible, I do my best to schedule surgeries in the spring and fall. Although my hip had gotten more painful, we scheduled the hip replacement for the first week of October.

I knew Dr. Logan had proven himself to be part of this large and growing orthopedic practice. He was young, extremely likeable, and took his time to fully explain the process of replacing my hip. With over 40 doctors in this group, there are multiple doctors specializing in every area of the body. Dr. Logan had an amazing background and received great training. I had no doubt he was the guy for this surgery. When I had my pre-surgery testing, I was also sent to a class that explained the dos and don'ts immediately after surgery and what to expect over the first few months. By the time surgery came around, I was more than ready to get it behind me. The pain greatly affected my sleep and how I walked.

The first thing that struck me when I awoke from surgery was the minimal pain I felt. I kept waiting for the pain to come, but it never did. The surgery went well, and Dr. Logan confirmed the hip joint desperately needed replaced. I felt I could go home that afternoon, but the surgeons felt it best for me to receive 24 hours of IV antibiotics due to the many infections I had in the past. I begged to go home that evening, but out of an abundance of caution, the surgeon decided to give me antibiotics overnight. I was given a walker at the hospital, but there was so little pain and I had little limitations when walking. I didn't feel I needed the walker. Pamala picked me up from the hospital the next morning and took me home to help me get settled. After helping me to get everything unloaded and into the house, she made a quick trip to the grocery store but not before asking if I would be okay. I told her I felt fine and could walk around the house without a lot of difficulty. I felt great and was glad to have the surgery behind me. All the pain from my hip was gone and I was excited about being able to get back to my normal routine. I did not use a walker or cane to walk once I arrived home. I felt much more stable when walking than before surgery and certainly felt less pain.

From experience, I always kept a small bag packed with a travel toothbrush, toothpaste, other toiletries, and a few articles of clothing. I sat on the side of the bed to clean and restock my hospital bag. I then removed all the clothing and took it to the washing machine. I began putting away other items when I felt something wet on my pants. My pants and shoes were covered in blood. I left a trail of blood from where I sat on the bed to where I was now standing. The incision opened and I was bleeding badly. The incision was on the front of my leg near where I had the major infection and 4"X4" of muscle had been removed. The skin in that area was paper thin and the staples used to close the wound had pulled through the skin, creating a gaping hole. I quickly sent a message to my wife and simply said, "you will need to pick up some hydrogen peroxide." Pamala knew in an instant that I had to be bleeding badly from somewhere. We normally kept hydrogen peroxide on hand, in both liquid and spray form, because I was always getting blood on something. She knew something had gone wrong when I told her that we needed more than we had on hand. Our master bedroom was covered in blood when she arrived home. The bathroom was bloody. Blood saturated towels and our bed sheets. Pamala said it looked as if a hog had been butchered in the bedroom. I am not sure she has seen a hog butchered, but that was her description!

The amount of blood I lost forced us to get to the hospital quickly. The surgeon cleaned the wound and replaced parts of the hip. I was given IV antibiotics and was told we could go home in a few days. When I got home this time, I took things much slower and was cautious about anything that would open the incision a second time. However, just a few days later, my leg became red, swollen, and warm to the touch. It was obvious I had an infection. We called Dr. Logan on a Sunday morning. He was at the hospital by the time we arrived. He had no option but to go back into my hip and perform the same procedure he performed just a few days prior. He cleaned the wound, replaced parts of the hip implant, and told me this time I would need to be in the hospital for an extended amount of time. After about a week of receiving constant IV antibiotics, my leg remained bright red and extremely swollen. Images and blood work were ordered to see how bad the infection had become. The surgeon needed to do a third procedure to clean and replace parts of the hip. My blood levels were low the day after the third surgery. I wasn't surprised. I lost a lot of blood during the past two surgeries. Having four surgeries over a few weeks also helped bring down my blood levels. I was frustrated because I had gone from doing so well the day after the original surgery to now. I had an infection and had gone through three additional surgeries. I had my first hip surgery in October, and it was early December. I had been in the hospital since October, and I wasn't sure when I could go home. My hip and leg were not healing, and the swelling did not dissipate. A team of doctors was formed to help deal with all the issues. After the fourth surgery, they told me if my leg didn't improve over the next couple of days, the only plan of action would be to remove all my hip replacement. They wouldn't be able to put a hip back in for at least three months.

It was now December and Christmas was just a few weeks away. One morning, the infectious disease doctor and others on the medical team decided I needed a fifth surgery in the following 24 to 48 hours. The plan was to remove the hip replacement metal and clean the bone. I would be on heavy antibiotics for months. It would be at least three months before the implants could be replaced.

"I know you are a man of faith," Dr. Logan told me. "If I was you, I would lean heavily on that faith."

Pamala and I prayed a simple prayer.

"God, we are in desperate need again for You to intervene and undertake so we don't need this procedure," we prayed. "We ask You, God, to give the doctors wisdom and give us patience and peace of mind. We put ourselves in Your hands and trust in You."

We were physically and mentally weak, and our faith was at an all-time low. I had been through four hip surgeries, a blood transfusion, and had been in the hospital for two months. We knew prayer was our only hope.

Prayer is simply communicating with an all- powerful God. It isn't about our strength, but His. The Bible tells us "He knows the way that I take."

Pamala later told me that she left the hospital room, went to the parking garage, and sat in the car to cry. While she sat in the car, a gentleman knocked on the car window. She wasn't sure what he wanted and hesitated to lower her window, but she did slightly and acknowledged him. He watched her get in the car and could tell she was going through a difficult experience. He asked if there was anything he could do to assist her. She told him no and said she had come to the car to get away from the room and collect her thoughts. He then reached in his pocket and pulled out a significant amount of cash and told her he felt God had impressed him to give her the cash. She tried to refuse it, but he insisted God had instructed him to give her the money and it was something he had to do. He promised to pray for the two of us, then walked back to his car and drove away.

Later that day, one of the doctors came in and was astonished by what he saw. He said my leg looked much better. He asked the other doctors to come by to see the vast improvement. One by one, each of the doctors came to my room. They individually agreed the redness was disappearing, the swelling was going away, and there was definite improvement. The doctors were amazed at the improvement over each 24-hour period. In two days, I improved enough that the doctors decided to wait for the surgery to remove my hip. I miraculously went home without surgery two days later. I followed up with Dr. Logan in his office a week later and he remarked how amazed he was at how well things had gone in such a short time.

I reminded him of his statement about me leaning on my faith.

A month later, I visited the same doctor. He requested that I speak to another hip-replacement patient about how I overcame problems with my implant. I agreed on the condition that I could talk about my belief in prayer. The surgeon not only agreed but had already explained to the other patient about my faith in God. After that, I talked to several other patients who were in the middle of great physical challenges. I witnessed to them about the power of prayer and how God gave me strength to get through problems and bring healing.

One passage I used is *John 14:1-4* where Jesus says, *"Let not your heart be troubled; you believe in God, believe also in Me. In my Father's house are many mansions; if it were not so, I would have told you. I go to prepare a place for you. And if I go and prepare a place for you, I will come again and receive you to Myself; that where I am, there you may be also. And where I go you know, and the way you know."*

First, Jesus says, "let not your heart be troubled." For me, this is easier said than done. Jesus spoke these words for the times when we find our hearts troubled or filled with fear. Jesus Christ became our mediator. Because His spirit now dwells in us, we can sit with Him in heavenly places spiritually during our greatest challenges. Psalm 23 says that in the very presence of our enemy, He would prepare a table for us. When we are under spiritual attack, we seldom feel like eating a large feast. However, when I go to God in prayer with the authority and power given me through the baptism of His spirit, I can sit in heavenly places and feast on the good things of God. The bread was always on the table in the Holy Place of the tabernacle. Jesus told us He is the bread of life. We can feast on His Word which is always there for us. His Word will fill the void, answer the questions, stop the doubt, and build our faith.

We may not have a physical hunger, but a spiritual hunger for His word will fill that place of void in time of trouble. We can go to God for our health, our marriage, our children, or our finances. We may not always get an immediate healing touch, but we can sit with Him in heavenly places and rest assured that everything will be all right. His Word will feed us so that there is no room for doubt to creep in and be a gateway for anxiety and fear. He is the great Shepherd. He knows what we need in the day of trouble and how to tend to our wounds. Christ Jesus took on flesh and walked on this earth. He was crucified and arose from the grave to give us more than just eternal life. He knew we would face hardships and times of great difficulty while here on earth. He knew we would need to sit with Him in heavenly places to get through those times of great hardship. I have sat with Him in those heavenly places while in the doctor's office, in a hospital room, and even in an MRI machine.

> I am not claiming to be someone with massive faith, but I have tapped into those heavenly places, hand in hand with my wife, as we went to God in prayer. We felt the

very shekinah glory of God settle on us as we faced challenges. I love to be in a great service and feel the move of God. Many times, Pamala and I have dragged ourselves into a service after facing a difficult week, only for the saints of God to begin praising the Lord. We soon find our feet tapping and hands clapping. Before we know it, our hands are raised to the Lord as we join fellow saints in praise.

It seemed like every Monday or Tuesday we'd face another negative doctor's report and attacks of the enemy came from nowhere. In those times, it would be great for our fellow saints gathered around us singing, or maybe the choir praising at full throttle, but that isn't possible. Sometimes, we have life come at us at the speed of light and we go from the high of a Sunday to the low of Monday. I have left a fabulous service on Sunday night only to be in the emergency room before sunrise Monday morning. The bills come in, the kids' clothes don't fit, the car breaks down, or the phone rings and the nurse says, "The test came back and the doctor needs you at the hospital in the next hour. Don't eat or drink anything from this point." We've learned we must first pull together as a husband and wife and go to the Lord in prayer.

I can't say our faith has always been great or we feel chill bumps as we begin to praise the Lord upon receiving a negative report. We often join hands and say a simple prayer that is barely audible at times. "God, You've been the fourth Man in the fire for us time and time again. You've shut the mouth of the lions over and over and we come to you once again needing you to move into our situation and make a way. Give us peace of mind and rest. Give patience and show us the way You desire us to take."

We ask God to bind the attacks of the enemy and to release both mental and physical healing. We've taken authority over the enemy coming against our home and watched the atmosphere change. I've told of a few times God did an instant work, but much of the time since my accident 40 years ago, it hasn't been instant. Still, we kept walking with God. As we moved forward, God took care of the problem one step at a time. As we kept walking, we saw God work. I believe our continued walking forward was the sign of faith God wanted and He worked and cleared the path. We wouldn't be here today if we stopped and said, "God when you put all this together and completely heal my body, we will serve You."

The Bible tells of those who were determined to get an answer from God. Due to their determination, they received an answer. The woman with the issue of blood had never seen anyone touch the hem of Jesus' garment and be healed, but she determined she would touch His garment and receive her healing. The four friends of the man who ripped a hole in the roof to lower their friend down to Jesus got what they came after. Had they said, 'The crowd is too large, we are too late, and we will wait for another more opportune time," their friend may have never received his healing. Had one of the four friends said, "No one has ever pulled the roof off before" or "We need to be proper and wait in line and if Jesus leaves, we can catch up to Him another day," they would not have seen their friend healed.

My trust in God is more than just in His ability to heal today. My trust is that I can sit with Him in heavenly places while the storm rages all around. He will be my peace, my strength, my joy, and the Captain of my ship so that He steers my life in the direction He desires. I find peace of mind when I sit in heavenly places with Him. While sitting in heavenly places, I find hope, strength, and the ability to carry on.

I'm a worrier by nature. I worry when things are going too well. It is not my nature to say, "Things will work out, so I'm not worried about it." I have had doctors tell me stressing over whatever I'm facing slows the healing process and hinders the body's natural ability to heal itself. It is hard for me to relax and not worry. More than anything else, there is something about my wife sitting next to my bed, not a word being spoken, but joining together in prayer that brings a great peace.

Chapter 17

COUNSELING BRINGS REVELATION

I didn't realize I developed a survival mechanism until week four or five of counseling. The pain management doctors required me to undergo counseling. Initially, I said nothing but my name and a little about my family. One counselor said he would catch up on paperwork if I was just going to sit there and stare at him. When I finally worked up the courage to open a bit, I mentioned my claustrophobia and how I hated it when the door to the exam room was closed! More than once, I had to redo an MRI because I moved too much during the exam. Anything on my face makes me nervous. The nurses often told me to stop taking the oxygen mask off my face.

My nightmares, my opening the doors of an exam room, as well as some of my other reactions were a way of escape, not wanting to be trapped. Often, we feel trapped by present circumstances, our past, or by things that happened beyond our control. I've talked to those who were physically and sexually abused as a child and felt trapped by what had happened. I'm not a counselor, but I know what it is to feel trapped by an accident that happened when I was a young man. I went from being one of the fastest runners on the field and a good ball player to finding it a struggle to walk, much less run.

One doctor said I lost the ability to judge the natural aging process. I tended to blame everything on my accident. If there was pain, it had to be related to my accident. I never thought it may be because I was getting older! This same doctor told me some of my problems were now due to the section on my driver's license under "date of birth" and not my accident. The average person suffers aches and pains as they age. I attributed all hurts and pains to October 18, 1982, and not to aging. I felt trapped by that one date. On several occasions, I have heard people say how they wish they could go back in time and redo a decision. If I could do things over, I would never have gone up on that scaffold. I would have stayed in bed that day. In fact, to be safe, I probably would have walked away from the job site long before October!

In counseling, we discussed how I felt trapped by the events of my accident; an accident which was not my fault, nor the fault of anyone else. No one could ever pinpoint why the scaffolding collapsed. The more we discussed the feeling of entrapment, I began to think of all the blessings I had in my life. I realized if I redid that one day, I would have missed some great experiences. Although I spent a lot of time in and out of hospitals, I was able to spend far more time with my sons when they were very young because I was always recovering from a surgery. The three of us spent a lot of days at home. I grilled hot dogs on our gas grill for their lunch, no matter the season. During the winter, I devised a way to grill without ever stepping outside. When we look back at old photos,

I'm almost always in some cast following some surgery, but I was there day after day with my sons instead of working a job. I would lie on the trampoline while they jumped. I watched them play in the backyard many days while recovering. Just about everything in our living room was broken and glued together because we played baseball, football, and basketball inside with me sitting on the floor. By the time they were six to 7 years old, they were very good because we had spent so much time playing baseball in the living room. My wife demanded we go outside after breaking a ceiling fan with a basketball.

I learned to drive with my left foot at a football stadium with a large parking lot. Therefore, I would drive to their elementary or middle school to have lunch with them. My wife and I found inexpensive ways of spending time together as a family. Those times were so enjoyable and unforgettable. My wife had a way of pulling things together so we would have a great time. We bought season tickets to Six Flags Over Texas, which allowed us to go to Fiesta Texas in San Antonio, Astroworld in Houston, and Six Flags in Dallas on the same season pass. At that time, the pass cost $200 for a family of four. That was a lot of money, but we could go to the three parks from March to December. My wife made lunch and took snacks. The boys learned we weren't buying food inside. I took a snack for each of the boys in my pockets and then we would go to the car for lunch. It was nothing big. It was as simple a trip as we could take, but the four of us had an enjoyable time and made memories we still laugh about today.

When we first started dating, Pamala hated the thought of riding a roller coaster. Now with two sons, she often was the one who rode with them while I waited on the ground below. For the sake of her family, she learned to ride roller coasters. More than 40 years later, one of the favorite things our 7-year-old grandson loves to do is ride roller coasters with his GiGi.

105

We found a campsite that was mostly empty during the week. It had showers and a great picnic and swimming area. We took the boys and let them run, swim, play, and have a blast. To them, that was as great as going to the Bahamas or some faraway place.

As I told my counselor all the things that I had been able to do with my family that I wouldn't have been able to do had I been working a job, I realized the accident allowed me to spend more time with my family. Even when I stayed in the hospital, the boys learned to enjoy staying there with my wife and me. One hospital often gave us a suite because I had been there so often and stayed for long periods. It sounds much more exclusive than it really is, but still it was nicer than a normal room. The main room was much like all the other hospital rooms but was a little larger with a few extras. Connected to the main room was a living room with a sofa that made into a bed and a large TV with a VCR or DVR and the ability to play video games. Our sons stayed with us on special occasions, including the night before the first day of school so I could see them in their new school clothes. They had birthday parties at the hospital. The nurses decorated the room with whatever they could pull together. We celebrated Thanksgiving, Christmas, and other holidays at the hospital. Christopher was disappointed one year because I wasn't in the hospital, and it was nearing his birthday. Brandon had a great birthday party at the hospital, and he wanted the same level of attention. I went in the hospital a few days before Christopher's birthday, and he was so excited to get the same decorations and treatment his brother enjoyed. The hospital was no longer a place they dreaded, but just another place where our family spent a lot of time. Though it wasn't the most enjoyable place to be, I spent much more time with my sons than most dads. And though I wish the accident had never happened, I would not trade these memories for any amount of money. My wonderful wife had a knack for pulling things together. She could put together a day or overnight trip on a very low budget and we were together as a family.

I no longer felt trapped by events of the past when I understood the blessings that the accident brought to my life. A lack of money and the need to be close to the hospital kept us from going far from home. We couldn't go on expensive vacations. We couldn't go to Disney. We couldn't buy the newest, latest toy, iPod, or things many of the other kids had. We could, however, provide a safe, secure home with love and care. Our kids didn't wear the newest Nike tennis shoes or name brand clothing, but they knew we loved and cared for them. They were blessed with a great network of friends and family. They spent a lot of time with my parents, my sister, Angela, and her husband Fred, and my brother, Richard, and his wife Gloria. They stayed with my in-laws, who lived five hours away, for two weeks each summer. I can't say I'm glad I was in an accident, but I must remind myself there are so many great blessings that have come with this. I cannot overlook how God has blessed my family. There have been some bleak and dark days, but there have also been many great enjoyable times. We must not fail to give thanks to God for the things He has done.

Chapter 18

BURNED

My condition constantly requires x-rays and MRIs. Because of my claustrophobia and constant pain, the best plan was to schedule the MRIs to be completed simultaneously at a hospital while under sedation. In the early 2000s, I had pain in several areas and needed multiple surgeries. In order to decide which surgery needed to be performed first, as well as explore some new lower back issues, arrangements were made with a local hospital near our home to have several series of MRIs done under sedation.

I've seen a massive change in MRI machines and procedures over the years. They started as extremely narrow tubes and the area from your head to the top of the tube extremely confining. I learned the best method was to close my eyes and not open them until the MRI was completed. For a while, several companies in the Austin area had goggles which allowed the patient to view a video. However, the goggles were expensive and easily broken. It became prohibitive for the imaging company to provide these goggles. Another device allowed patients to pick a radio station or play a CD while having the MRI. I liked to pick a CD and add up the time listed per song so I could know when I was getting to the end of the MRI. These days the tubes are larger, have much better lighting, and are well ventilated. Although there is more room, I've lost weight, and it is still a tight fit, I am glad when they are finished. Being sedated for an MRI is far more relaxing.

My wife sat with me until I was called back to get dressed. Then she left to run some errands. The radiologist and the anesthesiologist discussed the views needed, the best position for me to start in, and what the best plan would be. A young female assistant helped me transfer to the narrow scanning bed and wrapped me in a blue blanket.

I was assisted onto the sliding bed and watched as the anesthesiologist begin to administer the medications to sedate me. As I drifted off to sleep, the female assistant finished wrapping a blue blanket around me. The MRI uses magnets and radio wave signals which can cause heating and possible movement of some metal objects. I've carried a card for many years showing the type of implants I have so the radiology office can contact the makers of the various devices and surgical implants for MRI approval. Since I would be asleep and was having a series of MRIs performed, I was wrapped in this blue blanket to keep any bare skin from exposure to the sides of the scanner. My only thought as I went to sleep was which of my issues would need to be addressed first.

As I gained consciousness, I felt major pain in my right elbow. Not being able to open my eyes yet, I remember mumbling my arm hurt as if it had been dislocated. The nurse made a statement that even in my semi-conscious state struck me as odd. He said,

"Your arm isn't dislocated. We've already done X- rays of your elbow and the X-rays showed no signs of a dislocation." It was difficult to put together what was happening and being said.

I groggily opened my eyes and saw my arm on pillows and a lot of people around my bed. Doctors in surgical scrubs and lab coats and an unusual number of nurses were coming and going from my bedside. An elbow specialist rapidly barked orders while the radiologist talked softly to a lot of men in coats and ties and women in nice dresses.

I asked them what was going on and why I was in so much pain. They asked if I had a wound on my arm when I arrived at the hospital. I did not. They called Pamala and asked her the same question. The area was next to where the IV had been started in my arm. If there had been a large wound there, they would not have started the IV in that very spot. Had there been a pre-existing wound, the MRI probably never would have happened.

My arm felt like it had been burned by a hot stove. My elbow ached as if it had been dislocated. The elbow specialist asked if I was sure there was no wound on my arm before the MRI. I told him again that I did not have a wound upon entering the hospital. He then asked if I had any metal in my elbow that I had not told them about before the MRI. "No," I said. "My elbow is one of the few places in my body containing no metal."

I couldn't see my elbow because of the way it was positioned, and I couldn't reach to turn it so I could get a better view. I could tell my right arm was very swollen and red from the obviously injured area down to my hand. The specialist chose his words carefully and said there was a wound on my arm, but it wasn't too bad. He said they would watch my arm for a short while and would probably send me home before too long. I told them I was in a lot of pain and there was no way I would go home in that amount of pain. Someone needed to explain to me what had happened to my elbow during the MRI procedure!

I was taken from the recovery room into another area and seen by the emergency room doctor. She said they would wrap my arm in gauze, and I should just go home and call my orthopedic doctor the next day. I wanted to see the elbow specialist who was in the recovery room, but he had made it clear he wanted me to see the orthopedic doctor and wasn't interested in following my case.

It became crystal clear that something happened, and people attempted to separate themselves from what transpired as quickly as they could. I stayed in the hospital for a few days due to the amount of pain I was experiencing. When I arrived home, I unwrapped my arm bandages and could see ligaments and tendons, if not bone, in the mirror. There was a large hole at my elbow at least two and half to three inches across and deep. Later that night, the pain overwhelmed me, and the wound showed signs of infection. Since the injury occurred at this hospital, I felt I needed to go back there. When I arrived, they quickly took me back. Then they asked for my insurance

"Absolutely not," I said. "You guys did the damage and I'm not paying you to repair it."

There are times I should pray more before speaking! The ER doctor kept asking me what happened. "You tell me!" I kept saying. "It happened here at your hospital when I was getting an MRI."

He could have easily read the notes in the chart from the MRI to see what happened. I made a big enough scene and got a visit from someone in administration who apologized for asking for my insurance information or payment. I was then told the hospital would take care of all the costs related to my arm.

There are people in every hospital and most in large doctor's offices who are there specifically for the patient's benefit. The patient advocate or the caseworkers are wonderful people who fight on your behalf and give you answers when everyone else seems too busy. We've called for the patient advocate at all hours when there seemed to be no help in sight. I realized long ago that while I appreciate doctors and the nursing staff and admire their desire to help those in need, they are paid to do a job. Doctors are paid especially well to tend to their patients. If I placed my automobile in the repair shop and didn't receive satisfaction, I wouldn't hesitate to let them know there was still an issue with my car.

We send back a meal if it is not cooked right or the restaurant gets it wrong. We let every other industry know we aren't satisfied, except those in the medical field. For some reason, we hold doctors in such a high esteem that we are afraid to ask them questions or to complain if we feel we aren't receiving the needed treatment. My body is of far greater importance than my car or a meal I ordered.

At times, I wasn't given the opportunity to voice all of my concerns. The concerns I did express were tossed aside like a piece of wastepaper. Sometimes, a doctor talks so fast that I have no idea what is said. He'll be in and out in less than five minutes, only to send a bill later for the same amount as my car payment! After about two years into this journey, I began telling doctors to slow down. I was paying and they were getting paid. The one paying wasn't happy with the one getting paid! If they didn't have time to answer my questions and weren't concerned enough to see me as a patient, and not a number, it was best I find someone else who cared for me and my medical problems. I was more than a number. I was someone with a need. If I can't get satisfaction from physicians or feel they don't have time to talk, I am not going back.

I still didn't get a great explanation of what had happened and was sent home for the second time. Like before, we were home for only a few hours before we returned to the emergency room because of the pain and burning. Once again, the emergency doctor admitted me. This time, I asked for the orthopedic office I had previously gone to for all my orthopedic needs. This large orthopedic office had anywhere from 40 to 45 doctors on staff. The CEO of this large orthopedic group is my main orthopedic doctor. Although his specialty is knees, ankles, and feet, he had been kind enough to oversee whatever orthopedic needs I had. He would refer me to the doctor he thought would be the best physician in the group to address whatever my need.

When I was admitted to the hospital this time, I was given a large amount of antibiotics and started wound care several times a day. I was finally told what happened. In the process of moving me in and out of the scanner to check my vitals and to reposition me, the blue blanket wrapped around me moved enough to allow my skin to come in prolonged contact to the inside of the machine. Because I was under anesthesia, I didn't move when my arm got hot. It left me with second and third degree burns and a portion of the arm bone exposed. I basically cooked like a piece of meat in the skillet. I was inside the tube for about an hour. Doctors saw the arm wound after they brought me out.

I stayed in the hospital for several weeks. I felt better about my burn treatment when I was discharged. There was a plan for a follow-up visit in a week with a wound care office to treat my elbow. The wound began to get ugly just a few days after I arrived home, My arm was much more swollen and I was in a lot of pain.

When I arrived at the scheduled appointment, the physician's assistant (PA) said the doctor had been called out on a medical emergency. The PA was concerned about my arm. She took photos with her cell phone and sent them by text to the doctor. He immediately called her and said I needed to be admitted to the hospital to treat the wound. An infection had developed. The nerves in my arm were affected. I was told I would need long-term physical therapy after the wound healed. The wound care took several months of treatment and was extremely painful at first. I went to physical therapy for well over a year and still had tremors in my hand. I had trouble holding a pen or pencil. I also had trouble typing on a computer keyboard. Although the wound healed, pain still radiated down my arm into my hand. My fingers felt as if they were asleep.

The surgeon finally decided to clean the nerve from my elbow to my wrist. He made incisions at the elbow and wrist. After a few weeks of healing, we started over on physical therapy. This time, I could tell the difference and could tell my hand was getting stronger.

The MRI I never worried about turned out to be my biggest challenge. I've spoken to people about their fears of an MRI and most fear getting stuck in the tube. I am sure someone has gotten stuck, but I can't imagine it was for long. When I think of this period in our lives, I often think of how I have worried, not slept the night before an MRI, and become so anxious in the moments before getting on the table that my blood pressure was extremely high. However, nothing of any consequence came from all the exams I lost sleep over. It was the one I thought would go well that caused me major trauma. Such is life. There are things over which we worry and fret that never come to pass. Things often come out of nowhere. We can't go through life constantly worried about what may come our way. All my past worries and concerns were never about a burn, but about being trapped or stuck in that tube!

The Bible tells us His ways are above our ways and His thoughts above our thoughts. Long before the storm clouds gathered on the horizon of our lives, God knew the storm we would face and what we would need to sustain us. Long before my accident, God knew what I would encounter and had a plan for my life.

I'm the last one to say, "Just don't worry." It's difficult not to worry when the bills are due and the money is tight. It is difficult to not be concerned when there is talk on the job about potential layoffs or the doctor's report comes back negative. But I know I am God's child. If I turn to Him, I will "sit in heavenly places" spiritually. Paul wrote in Ephesians 2:4-6 *4 But God, who is rich in mercy, because of His great love with which He loved us, 5 even when we were dead in trespasses, made us alive together with Christ (by grace you have been saved), 6 and raised us up together, and made us sit together in the heavenly places in Christ Jesus.* I'm glad I serve a God who loved me long before I knew Him! He came and died not just so I could spend eternity in heaven, but so I can have abundant life here on earth. I don't believe that means God is concerned over me having a new Rolls Royce or a multi-million-dollar beach house, but I believe He does want me living a life of peace and joy, a life filled with hope, and an overcoming life.

An old song says, "I have hope, when things are not well with me, I have hope, a beautiful hope that has set me free." Doctors tell me not to worry which is almost like telling someone they cannot think of pink elephants! As soon as the statement is made, I can't help but worry. This is why being part of a local church body is so important. Prayers of the saints will lift you. A strong support group can pray and bring peace and strength. I would be less than honest if I said that I never worry, and I just put it in God's hands and go about my business. I learned that often many of the things that keep me up at night somehow come together in ways I never expected. Storm clouds will gather on the horizon whether I worry about them or not. When the wind blows and the thunder rolls, I pull my church family around me and do my best to put myself in the hands of a merciful God.

Chapter 19

MAJOR CHANGE

Pamala and I were blessed to be under the ministry of Pastor David Bernard and Pastor Rodney Shaw at New Life Church in Austin, TX. We were used in ministry and learned much under their leadership. Pastor Shaw met us at the hospital time and time again. Sometimes he was at the hospital before we arrived. He knew me well enough that he could tell the doctors what I needed if Pamala wasn't there. When Bro. Bernard was pastor of New Life Austin, he and Sis. Bernard helped us through a difficult spiritual time. We will forever be grateful to them for caring enough for us to meet with us on a weekly basis until we got through this challenging time. While we had a lot of longtime friends at New Life and loved the church, we felt God calling us to make a change, though we weren't sure what that meant.

We met with Pastor Shaw in November 2017 when he told us of three different options. One of those options was a daughter work just minutes from where we lived. This was in the most beautiful area of central Texas known as Dripping Springs, a small community west of Austin. We were excited about this opportunity to not just pastor a church, but also stay in the area that we currently lived. We had been involved in the schools when our boys were growing up. We worked in the general area and had looked at moving to the Dripping Springs area back in the late

1990s. Many close friends had moved to the Dripping Springs area to get outside of the city limits of Austin.

Though growth started to reach the Dripping Springs area, it still wasn't as crowded as Austin. This area is known as the gateway to the Texas hill country and attracts people from across the United States. Tourists visit the area for the many activities offered year around. It is only about a three-hour drive from Houston and about four hours from the Dallas/Ft. Worth area, so many come from these areas for a weekend getaway. In spring, people come for the beautifully colored wildflowers which includes an abundance of the state wildflower, the Texas bluebonnet. The hills and canyons are filled with blankets of bluebonnets and wildlife. Small towns like Johnson City, Marble Falls, and Wimberley are only a short drive from Dripping Springs. Each town has lots of unique shops and great restaurants. Dripping Springs alone has over 75 wedding venues. The hill country is called the wedding capital of the United States. For many years, it was known for its peach orchards, but it rarely made a profit. Once landowners switched from peach orchards to wine vineyards, they began to attract large crowds. The hill country is also known for its many barbecue restaurants, unique places to swim like Hamilton Pool and Jacobs Well, and tourists enjoy rafting or canoeing in the clear, cool waters of the many nearby rivers. In late fall, deer hunters fill every hotel and restaurant as they come to hunt on the numerous deer leases throughout the area. There are many venues that hold concerts every weekend. People can shop during the day and go to a concert at night.

In February 2018, we began pastoring the church in Dripping Springs and the Lord blessed us with a home in November. It was the fulfillment of a longtime desire and we felt doubly blessed to not have to leave our families or move away from the area we loved. The church was aware of the physical challenges I had in the past and they have pulled together during the times I've had to miss church for a surgery. We felt at home with the people and location instantly. Because of the rapid growth of the area, we felt we were in a prime place for a church to grow and we could be part of the community as it was springing to life. Our county has been one of the fastest growing counties for several years in a row and the growth shows no signs of slowing down as major companies continue moving into the Central Texas area.

Chapter 20

TO AMPUTATE OR NOT? THAT IS THE QUESTION!

Physically, there were two issues I knew needed to be addressed. I put both off as long as I possibly could. One of the problems was my right ankle and foot had gotten very painful and I was having serious lower back issues. The pain in the joints of my right foot and ankle had gotten to the point I was struggling to walk. I had a lot of broken hardware in my foot and where my right ankle was fused. The bone slowly grew so that my right foot was turned inward and rolled over. I walked more and more on the side of my foot. My orthopedic doctors referred me to many other doctors who specialized in the latest techniques for treating both ankles and feet. I was told over and over that an artificial ankle would not be an option because there was not enough bone to hold the hardware in place. Furthermore, once the hardware came out of place, I would be forced to have an amputation.

Over and over, doctors told us that an amputation just below my right knee was the best solution. My orthopedic doctor went so far as to set up an appointment with a couple of amputees who were active afterward. One of those men had been in a motorcycle accident. Another was injured in Desert Storm. Both men had no choice because the decision for amputation was made during surgery. Neither man had suffered for a long time like I had, which meant phantom pain wasn't as programmed into their brain as it was in mine. Several physicians said my pain had gone on for such a long period of time that it was part of my memory. They weren't sure how long I would have phantom pain. In fact, several doctors told me the phantom pain could last as long as 10 years or more. I could not bring myself to consider amputation. It seemed too final. My wife encouraged me to have the amputation because she knew the constant pain I felt when I walked.

The amputees spoke of phantom pain, but it had not lasted long. One man ran a marathon a year after his amputation. I still could not bring myself to consider an amputation because I thought about how often I awoke each night to get up and walk around the house before I can go back to sleep. I couldn't imagine putting on a prosthetic each time I got up from bed. I had been shown how well advanced the prosthetics were, including the ability to adjust to a small pebble when walking. All the amputees with whom I visited said they had adjusted, but I just couldn't wrap my mind around the permanency of an amputation. I have known for over a decade that day may come, but I wasn't ready for it.

In September 2016, I had a large bone growth removed from the bottom of my foot. This started out as a small bone spur but grew larger and caused a lot of pain over an eight-month period. Finally, the surgeon scheduled a surgery to remove this bone growth. The growth was larger than he had expected.

He removed several other bone spurs once he opened the bottom of my foot. A year later, in September of 2017, he performed almost the same surgery, but the growth was larger and had more bone spurs. This time, he ordered radiation to keep the growth from returning. He said he had never seen a return of that type of bone growth after radiation. Exactly a year later, in September of 2018, he removed an even larger growth and many bone spurs. He also removed a broken metal plate as well as several pins and screws. Several of the larger screws broke when he attempted to remove them. After the doctor discharged me, I returned to the hospital. The pain was more than I could take.

My foot was extremely swollen and painful. It took several weeks before I could wear a walking boot. The arthritis became so severe in the small joints of the foot that every step was painful. With my foot rolled inward, walking was a struggle. The surgeon insisted I reconsider an amputation. I visited several additional surgeons and they all felt there was no option but amputation. One orthopedic surgeon said it looked as if I had fallen through the roof of a Home Depot and landed on a shelf of screws because I had so much hardware in my right foot! There were broken screws and pins in my foot. I was told it would probably do more damage to remove the broken hardware than just leaving it in place. I reached a point where my right foot was so bad only a couple of doctors would even make an appointment with me.

I scheduled an appointment with one highly recommended orthopedic surgeon. I knew if he saw the x-rays before I arrived, he probably would tell me he wouldn't see me because there was no option but amputation. He ordered x-rays and I waited in an exam room for about 20 minutes. Finally, this young surgeon walked in with a handful of recently taken x-rays. He showed them to me and then called in the nurses and other doctors in his office to come and look at my x-rays. He told his medical team that my ankle and right foot was so severe he wanted everyone in his office to see something they may never see again. As the exam room filled, I wasn't sure how to take my images being the amusement of the office staff. He then asked me which doctors had done most of the surgeries. I told him I would rather not say until he told me what he felt he could do for me. The orthopedic surgeon then said that there was nothing further he could do, but an amputation. He said since this had been an ongoing issue, I would have worked my way to one of two orthopedic doctors in the Austin area. Sure enough, one of the two doctors he named was my main orthopedic doctor.

Prayer was my only hope. My wife and I joined in prayer for God to heal my right foot, or take away some of the pain, or open a door to a physician that could make an improvement. In 2019, one of my original orthopedic surgeons came out of retirement. I made an appointment with him. After looking at all that had been done since I had last seen him over a decade before, he referred me to Dr. Mark Brinker at the Texas Orthopedic Hospital in Houston Medical Center. I had a very low level of expectation, but not because I doubted Dr. Brinker was a great surgeon. I had been to many "best of the best" physicians who told me an amputation was necessary. We prayed for God to open a door, and He did. This was early in 2020.

By the time we arrived in Houston, Covid-19 started making the news. Stories of hospitals filling up were becoming common. This hospital only saw orthopedic cases, so it wasn't as affected by Covid. We arrived at the hospital and went through all the Covid protocols. We were taken to a waiting room where I saw what appeared to be babies no more than a month or two old who had just undergone major orthopedic surgery. There were people in wheelchairs who had all types of orthopedic devices I had never seen. When we were taken back to the x- ray area, I had a full scan of the length of both legs, and then we were taken to an exam room. After a few minutes, in walked Dr. Brinker. To say he had an air of confidence is an understatement. He wasn't arrogant. He was quite friendly but was extremely confident and spoke at a machine gun pace to his physician's assistant. I felt sorry for her as she tried to take notes on what he was saying. He asked a few questions and then said he had spoken to my surgeon in Austin on several occasions to get an idea of what I was experiencing.

"I can help you if you are willing to endure the treatment that is needed," Dr. Brinker said.

He said my right foot and ankle was as bad as he had ever seen, but if I was willing to endure a long period of recovery, I would be able to walk much better when he was done. He said my right leg was three quarters inch shorter than my left leg because of all bone that had been removed. My forefoot was turned inward, and the ankle had rolled badly. For several years, I had worn out shoes in a matter of months. We paid for expensive shoes, handmade shoes, and shoes with all types of soles, but the right shoe would be worn out in three to four months. It would be worn badly on the side and would become uncomfortable to wear.

The procedure involved breaking my right ankle all the way across so that Dr. Brinker could lengthen my right leg using an Ilizarov Fixator. After my leg was the proper length, the device would slowly turn my forefoot in place. Once that stage was completed, the same device would gradually flatten my foot. Dr. Brinker estimated it would mean wearing the device for five to six months to make the needed adjustments. We returned several weeks later for Dr. Brinker to take measurements for the fixator. He built the fixator and placed the device on my leg much like it would be after surgery. He wanted to make sure I was up to the surgery and willing to wear the device for as long as it would take. The device alone cost about $75,000 so I had to be sure that I was willing to risk infection and wear this large metal cage on my leg for the duration. I felt I was ready to move forward. Dr. Brinker's nurse told us he only accepted patients who everyone else had given up on.

He despised amputations and would do whatever he could to avoid an amputation. The surgery was scheduled a month later in May 2020.

On the day of the surgery, we met a young lady who appeared to be in her early 30s and who had a fixator in the same place I would wear mine. We asked her about her experience and saw she was walking well with the device. She was there to get her device removed after having it on for about five months. She was glad she had the surgery. She said the first six weeks were extremely painful, but it was worth it in the end. Shortly after talking to this young lady, I was called back. When I awakened from surgery, I was in a lot of pain. There were 13 rods going through my lower leg bone to hold the 3 metal plates surrounding my leg in place. They would aid in helping make the needed adjustments.

On the second day, nurses showed my wife how to clean each rod and replace the sponges on the rods next to the skin. I stood up for the first time and the pain in my leg was immense. There was a lot of pressure around each of the rods. The plates were so large that I had to hold my right leg away from the left leg. Pamala bought a pair of basketball warmups that buttoned all the way down each side. We bought two pairs of brown pants and two pairs of blue pants. A lady in our church made a bell bottom type pant leg large enough to pull over the plates easily. I was released from the hospital three days after surgery. I was still concerned about the long period of time I would wear the fixator. I was told I would walk with the device after about two months, but it was already proving difficult to sleep with it on. Moving was cumbersome and we were just getting started!

I'm thankful God has a way of speaking to reassure us that He is in control. On the way home, I was hungry for something other than hospital food. I was in the back seat of our SUV and randomly pulled up places to eat on the way out of Houston. A mom-and- pop hamburger restaurant popped up on Yelp and we decided to stop there to eat. Everyone stared at the fixator and a few people groaned. A lady introduced herself to us as the owner of the restaurant. She asked if we had been to an appointment with Dr. Mark Brinker. That was a shock because Houston is the fourth largest city in the United States and has some of the largest hospitals in America. The medical center alone is larger than most downtown areas. Of all the doctors in Houston, for her to ask about Dr. Brinker seemed odd. She pointed to her son who was in his early 30s. When her son was approximately 10 years old, he fell at school and had his arm extended with his hand on the ground. A very large boy ran and jumped on him, accidentally landing on her son's elbow. An ambulance took him to Texas Children's Hospital in Houston Medical Center. Several doctors examined his severely crushed elbow, but none of the surgeons were sure how to put his elbow back together so he wouldn't lose use of his arm. One of the physicians suggested contacting Dr. Brinker. After wearing one of the fixators for four to five months, he regained full use of his arm. She reassured us that we would be glad that Dr. Brinker performed the surgery. God led us to this small hamburger restaurant, surrounded by many of the popular chain hamburger fast food restaurants, and allowed us to be encouraged by someone who had gone through what we would face over the coming months.

Jesus said in Luke 12:6-7 *"Are not five sparrows sold for two copper coins? And not one of them is forgotten before God.* **7** *But the very hairs of your head are all numbered. Do not fear; therefore, you are of more value than many sparrows."* (NKJV). We know this verse isn't about sparrows or the number of hairs on our head, but it is to tell us how important we are to God. At any given time, there are approximately 1.5 billion sparrows on the earth. Sparrows have a short life span. We go throughout the day without even noticing the sparrows. Jesus said five sparrows were sold for two coins. Sparrows were not expensive to purchase. God values all his creations, even something as small as the sparrow. Of all his creations, we are His most valued creation. Many sparrows were sold daily in the marketplace for a few copper coins. They were so small they weren't sold individually. They were sold in groups of five at a time. Jesus said, "I see every sparrow that falls." As a child of God, I am far more valuable than a sparrow.

Life doesn't always go like the believer thinks it should, but He is watching over us. His hand is on us, and He is walking with us every step of everyday. God knows my daily needs. He knows the sleepless nights and the days that I feel as if I can barely put one foot in front of the other. He knows when I am up, and He knows when I am down. He knows when I feel life is closing in on me and what I need to sustain me. God knows my every problem and every storm I will face in the future. The number of hairs on our heads is constantly changing, yet He knows how many hairs are on my head. Even more importantly, He knows everything in my life that occurs. He knew it was going to occur long before I saw it coming. Serving God does not mean I will have smooth sailing the rest of my life, free of anxiety, fear, problems, or tests. When I'm not sure the sun will ever shine again, I know that I am important to God. He cares for me, and He is watching out for me. Past challenges may have left us scared or feeling damaged, but we are still important to God.

Pamala searches for antiques that are in great shape. She is always on the lookout for unique pieces. Every now and then, a piece has a story that adds to its value. God sees our story and He knows what we've been through. In these times, we draw closer to Him.

We are each a unique work made by the Master Craftsman. It is amazing to know that I am so special to the One who created everything in the vast universe. I am so important to Him that He had a design for my life from the very beginning.

While I worried about an amputation, my God aligned things so I could reconnect with a doctor I had not seen in years. This doctor sent me 200 miles away to a doctor who could perform the needed repairs all the other doctors deemed impossible. Then to reassure us, God guided us to someone who could show us the result of this doctor's work. I don't think it was coincidence Pamala and I stopped at that specific restaurant.

We had talked to the young lady at the hospital while waiting for surgery, and now after the surgery, we were able to speak to someone else who knew what we were facing. I'm thankful I am important to the Lord and He cares for me. My hopes rise and my faith grows when I begin to think I am of value to the King of Kings and the Lord of Lords. He valued me so much that He directed me to someone who could sit down and share their story with me so that I would be at peace with what I was going through.

I returned to Houston every week for two months and then monthly through the end of the year. About a month out from the original fixator placement, the nurse taught my wife how to adjust the device so that it would extend my leg. She adjusted the pins to three times a day. Each visit, leg measurements were taken to determine the next set of daily adjustments. When my leg reached the desired length, we began turning my foot into place. This process took two months. Once my right foot moved into place and the leg length reached, we waited for the bone to heal. The bone had to grow to fill in the three-quarter inch space between the leg bone, as well as heal from being turned into place.

The lady I spoke with before going into surgery was correct about how painful the first six weeks would be. It was extremely painful each time I stood. Slowly, the pain subsided. The rods that went through my right leg constantly cut my left leg. I tore pants that had been made for me. I also ripped holes in the sheets and bedding while sleeping. My wife was faithful in cleaning the 13 rods daily. Since the rods went all the way through my leg, that was 26 areas that needed cleaning and 26 sponges that had to be placed on the rods.

When my foot reached the proper alignment, we focused on flattening my foot from the rolled position. I started walking with the external fixator in August. Dr. Brinker said walking encouraged the bone to heal. He expected the fixator to be removed in October. Unfortunately, in mid-September, Dr. Brinker felt the bone was growing too slowly and ordered a series of lab work. The results showed I was low on vitamin D. He prescribed a diet high in iron and vitamin D. The bone growth continued to be slow. I went to each appointment expecting a surgery date to remove the fixator, but it kept being postponed.

Finally, the fixator and 13 rods were removed in late January. I was on crutches until the holes from the rods filled in. Dr. Brinker said if I walked on my leg too early, the leg bone would splinter, and I would be forced to undergo an amputation. The wait for the holes to heal seemed to take forever. It wasn't until March 2021 that I was finally given permission to walk without crutches. The broken hardware and arthritis still caused pain in my foot, but it was great to no longer walk on the side of my foot. I was thankful we had not chosen an amputation and that God heard our prayer.

Sometimes, it seems as if all of hell puts a bullseye on you or your family. As if one large trial isn't enough, the trials or tests of faith come like waves crashing on the beach. You get hit by one trial and then another comes crashing in on you. Experiencing a trial while in the middle of another trial can cause us to wonder if we can withstand all that comes crashing around us.

Chapter 21

TRAGEDY STRIKES AGAIN

About the same time, Dr. Brinker sent orders for me to follow up with a hematologist to oversee the blood work showing several deficits that explained the slow bone growth. Pamala and I faced yet another one of the greatest trials of our life. In 2020, we were excited that our son Chris and his wife Danielle were expecting their second child. We were glad Levi would have a sibling. Most of all, we were excited we would have a fourth grandchild. When we found out they would have a girl, we were even more excited because our family is known for boys. My wife came from a family of girls. Brandon was the first boy in her family in over 30 years. We had two sons. Our first two grandchildren were boys and the third grandchild a girl. We had three grandchildren born in three years. It had been a couple of years since we had a new grandchild born.

Chris and Danielle travelled as full-time evangelists, but they have a home just six houses down from us. We love when they come home to Dripping Springs. Their son, Levi, is a joy to be around. Though I struggled with my leg not healing fast enough, I had something to look forward to when it did heal. Chris and Danielle left to visit Danielle's parents in Portland and would stay there through Thanksgiving and be back to spend Christmas with us. Danielle's pregnancy was around 20 weeks when they left for

Portland. I received a frantic call from Chris saying Danielle was in labor. I thought they would give her something to delay the contractions, so I didn't give it a lot of thought. Little did we know how bad Danielle was because she didn't want to have us worry. She delivered Sancy Reigh at 24 weeks. This perfectly formed beautiful girl was put on tubes and machines. She weighed a little under two pounds, but she was doing well according to the doctors. Sixteen days later, the Friday after Thanksgiving, the doctors told Chris and Danielle that Sancy was doing as well as could be expected but would remain in the hospital until March, which is when she was originally due to be born.

Early the next morning, Chris called and said that something was wrong. The hospital called for them to get to the hospital immediately. Sancy stopped breathing and died. Due to Covid, Chris and Danielle were the only ones allowed in the hospital, so we did not go to Portland when she was born. Chris and Danielle held Sancy every day in the hospital before her death. When doctors removed all the tubes and disconnected the machines, Chris and Danielle held Sancy for the first time without any medical devices connected to her.

My wife and I immediately scheduled a flight to Portland. We got there a few minutes before the funeral home arrived at the church and the funeral planning began. Since Chris and Danielle's marriage, we have grown close to her family. They are some of the most giving and caring people we've ever met. They made a meal every evening for their family and ours. It was comforting being with their family and having them share our grief. We saw Sancy for the first time in her coffin at the funeral. What a difficult way to meet your granddaughter! Her funeral was one of the most difficult things I've ever experienced. Watching your son go through something you can't help with is very tough. To meet your granddaughter for the first time in a coffin is not how it is supposed to be.

Chapter 22

MANAGING AND GIVING THANKS IN THE STORM

I felt like the Psalmist who wrote, Psalm 73:1-3- *1"Truly God is good to Israel, To such as are pure in heart. 2 But as for me, my feet had almost stumbled; My steps had nearly slipped. 3 For I was envious of the boastful, When I saw the prosperity of the wicked"* (NKJV). This Psalm is attributed to Asaph. He was known as a singer, a musician, a prophetic composer, as well as a leader of the temple choirs for David and very likely for Solomon. In this Psalm, he poses a question many have asked. He starts by saying God is good to Israel. We can all testify that God is good to His people. Anyone who has served God for any length of time can tell of God's goodness, of His mercy, and of His grace. The very fact He died for our sins, arose on the third day, and took back the keys to death, hell, and the grave for us, is worth more than anything I deserve. Before He ascended, He promised to return in the form of the Holy Spirit. For the first time, He would not be in the Holy of Holies where only a priest could experience the glory of God, nor would He be walking in flesh among man. For the first time, He would dwell in the hearts of men and all of mankind could experience the baptism of His spirit. That is a great blessing not just for the people who are currently filled with his Spirit, but this was for "whosoever will." Everyone has access to this great promise.

When Peter stood up on the day of Pentecost, he responded to those who asked the question, "What must we do?" They asked what they needed to do to receive this great promise. Peter told them to simply repent of their sins, get baptized in the name of Jesus by immersion for the remission of sin, and then God will come down and baptize you with His spirit and fill your heart with the glory that once only resided in the Holy of Holies (Acts 2:38). The word "shekinah" is an English translation of a Hebrew word which means "settling" or "dwelling." The glory of God settled on the mercy seat of the Ark of the Covenant in the Holy of Holies compartment in the Tabernacle.

God's spirit now settles and dwells in man's heart, no longer in a single location. We are blessed to have access to the glory of God no matter what our background may be and no matter what past generations of our family may have done. It isn't dependent on being rich or poor, educated or uneducated, but it is dependent upon simply repenting of your sins and telling God you no longer desire to live the life you have lived, and you want Him to be in control of your life. When you are baptized in the name of Jesus, your sins are remitted and take on the powerful name of Jesus. He then fills you with His spirit and dwells in your heart. Wherever I may be, He is always with me. He no longer lives in temples made of hands but dwells in the hearts of men. What a glorious blessing this is!

When the Psalmist says, "I know you are good to your people, to those of a pure heart," he is testifying that he has seen God's hand of mercy on His people. In the very next verse, Asaph makes a statement most everyone has asked at some point. He says, "but as for me, my feet almost stumbled, my feet almost slipped." I know God blesses and watches out for His people, but I go through great trials that cause my knees to buckle under the weight and strain of the burden! The load can seem so great that I have trouble standing and my feet seem to slip. I am not talking about walking away from God or giving up on God. For me, there is no other hope but God. To walk away from God would be to turn my back on my only hope to overcome great trials. Asaph is saying, "I was in a bad place. In fact, I was in such a bad place in my life my feet almost slipped. The enemy seemed stronger than I was, and he outnumbered me. I was struggling to stand, much less walk, because I felt as if I was the very focus of hell itself."

During trials, it is easy to look around at those who are not even trying to live for God and begin to take note of their lives. It seems as if everything they touch turns to gold and they appear to be living a great life. They are the ones who get the raise or promotion on the job. They have new cars or homes, and their children seem to be the ones who get all the breaks. When we are in a trial that weighs us down

and causes us to almost stumble, it can be easy to look at those who only attend church on Christmas or see others who make little effort to live for God, although they may have been raised in and around the church. They seem to be far more blessed than you, even though you attend church every time the doors are open, are faithful in your giving, and volunteer for every area of the church. It is then that we respond like Asaph and become envious of the foolish. We see their prosperity. They seem like they are strong while you are in a great struggle.

Right after I believed that I would bounce back quickly and be good as new once I had a couple of surgeries and a little physical therapy. As the surgeries began to pile up, it dawned on me that my life was forever changed. I realized I could no longer do some of the simple things I enjoyed doing, such as going for a jog or playing on our church softball team. I struggled just to learn how to walk again. I began asking God why I was going through this great struggle. I was far from perfect, but I was at the church just about every day. I worked my construction job and then Pamala and I would be at the church in the evening because we were youth pastors. We taught a Sunday School class. I mowed the church lawn, which was over two acres. My wife worked as my dad's secretary at the church. We were involved in every area of the church. By the time we got home after Sunday morning service and lunch, it was close to 2 p.m. We were back at church at 4:30 for choir practice to prepare for Sunday night. It was late when we got home after Sunday night service.

We gave our lives to the church and to God. As a very young man, I found myself facing a lifetime of medical challenges. I almost stumbled and my feet almost slipped as I looked at so many who walked away from God and yet, by all appearances, were greatly blessed. I harbored bitterness and was upset with God for allowing the accident to happen. I had every excuse to stay home from church. It was a struggle just to get dressed and get in the car. I felt a great deal of pain by the time the service was over. It took stamina just to sit through a service, yet I was there every service.

I was in this state of mind when we decided for the second time to return to the condominiums where my accident had occurred. I am not sure why we went back there. It was as if we were drawn back to that spot. When we arrived, we stood in the exact spot I landed, and I fussed at God. "Why, God? You could easily have kept me up on the scaffolding and not allowed me to fall! Why, God, would you allow this to happen to me? Why, God, when there are mass murderers in the world or those who commit other horrific crimes yet have perfect health, would you take away my health? I was doing all I could for you!" Pamala and I brought people to church. We did outreach consistently. We gave our lives to serving the Lord with everything we had! Why, God, would this happen to us? We've watched many families completely turn their backs on the church and yet they have been blessed financially. They are blessed in their home and their family. Their finances seem to be blessed. Why not mine?

I stood there fussing at God for a long time. When I finally got it all out, I stood there silently for a few moments with my wife quietly holding my hand. I thought of how blessed I was to have her, how God had spared my life in that very spot, and how I should have died, but I was alive. Now, instead of fussing at God, I found myself giving Him thanks. "Thank you, God, for my family. Thank you, God, for my wife who has been by my side faithfully, never once complaining about all that she had to take on. Thank you, God, for the times the doctors had been surprised when I walked out of the hospital."

As I began to praise the Lord for His blessings, I found there was far more for which to be thankful than to be upset at God about. My outlook changed by the time I got back in the car. We returned every year and sometimes several times a year to praise and thank God. There was something about going and standing in that spot, pouring our hearts out to God, telling Him my feelings and how I was upset with how He handled things.

Inevitably, I would begin to praise God for all He had done in my life. I thanked God for healing and listed all the things He had done for me. I thanked Him for letting me see my sons' birth and watch them grow up. The list of things God had done in my life grew as we experienced infections so bad the doctors didn't think I would make it. God intervened!

Now, many years later we faced the trial of our lives. Our granddaughter lived for just 16 days, and we didn't get to see her until the day of her funeral. Some may not agree with me fussing at God, but I believe I can share with God what I experience and feel. At that point, I had logged over 80 major surgeries and countless day surgeries. I spent months at a time in the hospital. I hurt 24 hours a day. We had just been told there were potentially serious issues found in my blood work. Dr. Brinker was concerned about the possibility of an infection before the bone completely healed. While dealing with all of this, we were hit with the loss of a granddaughter. We watched our son and daughter-in-law be broken by the loss of a child. We planned the funeral for a 16-day-old baby. "God, why? I am stumbling, my feet are slipping, and I am not sure I can hold up under the weight of this trial."

Pamala and I dealt very differently with Sancy's death. The morning Sancy died, Chris called by FaceTime so we could see her without all the tubes and machines. Chris and Danielle held her for six hours before the hospital staff took Sancy. I went to my wife's shop and opened it for her because I needed to do something. I couldn't sit still. Pamala couldn't go to her shop and face people. She was too broken and crying. In fact, she asked why I wasn't crying. I was in a daze. I was stunned and not sure it had completely hit me. As the day went on, I cycled through the various emotions of unbelief, anger, great sadness, and back to unbelief.

In Psalm 73:16, Asaph says, *"Until I went into the sanctuary of God; then I understood their end."* (NKJV)

Asaph argued that he cleaned his heart and did what he felt was his best but grew angry because it seemed like the wicked were blessed while he was in a struggle. He knew God blessed His people and he was part of the people of God, but he was going through a time when he felt as if his feet may have slipped. Then he says, *"when I went into the house of God I understood."* There is nothing greater in this life than the church, not a building of brick and mortar, but THE Church, the people of God. Nothing will sustain you like the church. I don't understand why struggling people don't turn to the church. I am not sure how they make it. I have walked into the house of God broken. I have been crumpled by life and it took everything I had to put one foot in front of the other. When I walked into the house of God, both as a member of the church and as pastor, and when the people of God began to sing His praises and exalt the name of the most high God, my load grew lighter and I gained understanding that He was with me. I am not forgotten or alone. I am part of the blessed people of God, and I was lifted by their worship and praise. Asaph said, "When I got to the house of God and I put my focus on Him, I no longer focused on my pain or my brokenness. My focus was on God who will sustain and keep me. He will give me peace of mind and cause me to rest."

I've gone to a church prayer meeting in so much pain, worry, and anxiety that I couldn't focus well enough to offer much of a prayer. As I sat or even laid on the church floor in pain, I began to receive strength and encouragement. When I left, my problem wasn't resolved, but I realized that I wasn't in this battle alone. The church prayed for me, and I had God on my side. I may have felt alone and felt as if I didn't matter to God when I arrived, but the load was lighter when I left, and my feet were firmly planted and no longer slipping. I'm glad I'm going to more than a building where traditions are upheld. I surround myself with people who know how to call on a God who overcame death itself, and then the word of God is preached. The word of God is forever settled and sure. When the anointed preached Word of God goes forth, my load is lifted, I find myself saying, "Amen!" I clap and lift my hands because the Word of God is like a two-edged sword that will cut away the doubt, anxiety, and fear. The preached Word of God will bring strength and build faith.

Before I became a pastor, there were times I went to church and had to lie down on the floor in the back or in a church office where I could listen to the service. I was in too much pain to sit on a pew, but I wanted to be as close to the people of God as I possibly could. I can't explain it, but when I left, I felt encouraged and knew everything was going to be all right. I didn't know how, but I knew God would work it all out.

Asaph recounted a time he stumbled and almost fell. He got his eyes on the wicked who seemed to be more blessed than he was, though he lived for God, and he served David as the choir leader. In Psalm 73:23-28, he changes his whole outlook. The final six verses should encourage every child of God. *"Nevertheless, I am continually with You; You hold me by my right hand. You will guide me with Your counsel, and afterward receive me to glory. Whom have I in heaven but You? And there is none upon earth that I desire besides You. My flesh and my heart fail; But God is the strength of my heart and my portion forever. For indeed, those who are far from You shall perish; You have destroyed all those who desert You for harlotry. But it is good for me to draw near to God; I have put my trust in the Lord God, That I may declare all Your works."* (NKJV)

Asaph says, "God I've made up my mind that I am staying with you and as long as I hold to you, I know you will hold me in Your right hand." We know God is a spirit. The right hand of God is His power and authority. Asaph says, "No matter what, I will hold onto God because His power will hold me." My God has all power and all authority. His name is above whatever may come against me. Hell may attack with everything it has, but if I remain in the hands of God and run to the strong tower that is the name of Jesus, the enemy cannot do anything to me that God doesn't give him permission to do. God will guide me and watch over me.

Sadness still washes over me when I think about that beautiful baby girl who was perfect in every way. She had the cutest long blonde eyelashes and her little fingers with tiny fingernails were perfectly formed. Tears come to my eyes when I think about never seeing her first bite of real food, her first steps, or never playing with her or watching her play and laugh with our other grandchildren. But as Asaph said, if I draw near to the Lord and serve Him, there is far more to it than this life. I will see her again in Heaven and I will be with her in the land where no baby has ever died. I will play with her. I will have a new body and will not be limited like I am in this life. I put my trust in God. I am hopeless without Him. Without the people of God to help hold me up in those times that my feet are slipping, I am not sure how I would get out of bed somedays. I have sat with many who seem blessed, but who either don't serve God or have walked away from God. When they faced a great trial and told me their struggles, they say how sad they were they didn't have a church to attend and worship the Lord. Those who never experienced God and didn't know the simplicity of prayer felt as if they couldn't call on God because of the life they lived. They spoke of feeling alone and felt they had no place to turn.

Since the death of Sancy, I've fussed at God at times and said, "Okay God, I'm not sure what you are doing or why this is happening." When I list the many things God has done for me, an old song comes to mind. "When I think of the goodness of Jesus and all He has done for me, my soul cries out, hallelujah, praise God for saving me."

Chris and Danielle stayed in Portland until the end of the year, but they were blessed by many friends they met while evangelizing. Several pastors offered them a place to get away from everything until they could move forward. They attended a wonderful church in Florida where they stayed for several months and received healing offered by close friends with wise counsel. To show how faithful God is to those who hold to Him,

God blessed them with a healthy baby boy named Jaxon in February 2022. He is a big baby boy with lots of hair and has won over our hearts with his broad grin and sweet demeanor. He is precious and we are so glad God allowed Danielle to go full term, even though the doctors watched her and were concerned she may not be able to do so.

God is good. I have no reason to walk away from Him. Where would I go? What else could I lean on that would be as sure as the rock Christ Jesus? I know He wants the best for me. While I don't understand the whys of this life, I know who is in control and I know if I hold to Him, He will hold me in the power of His right hand. In the end, we are headed to a land of milk and honey if we continue serving Him.

I felt so underdressed for Sancy's funeral because I could not wear a suit. I could only wear a dress shirt and pants specially made to fit over the three metal rings around my leg. I wore the external fixator 24 hours a day. It could not be removed.

I was eager to have the surgery to remove the fixator upon my return from Portland because I had gone eight months with it on my leg. I could only wear my left shoe and a specially made walking shoe with Velcro on the right foot during that time. I wore only three different pairs of pants because that was all that would fit over the metal rings. The surgery went smoothly, and we only had to stay in the hospital overnight so they could give me IV antibiotics for a 24-hour period. When the nurse discharged me, I put on a pair of regular pants and both shoes. It felt great to be dressed normally!

Chapter 23

RESPITE

I returned to see Dr. Brinker on a weekly basis for the first month. The hope was that I could walk without crutches by late February. By mid-February, it was evident the holes in the bone were closing slower than expected. I was impatient and ready to walk without the crutches. Dr. Brinker said if the bone splintered there would be nothing to do but to amputate my leg. We came too far for that to happen at this point. There was little pain in my leg and foot, and it was very tempting to walk, but the fear of the bone splintering kept me on my crutches.

Finally, in late April of 2021, Dr. Brinker said I could start walking without fear of the bone splintering. My leg looked like it had been shot with buckshot because the rods left round scars. Nevertheless, I was glad to walk. Even better, for the first time in years, I walked straight and not on the side of my right foot! I also noticed the new length of my right leg made a big adjustment in my stride and helped my lower back.

Pamala and I resumed our daily walks. I knew I would need to work up to our routine of walking well over three miles a day. Our home is near the top of a hill. We began walking our most popular walk, starting out uphill. I made it about a half a mile before working my way back home. I was weak and had lost stamina I fought so hard to gain. Nevertheless, we committed to our daily walk. In six to seven weeks, I could walk a full three miles without a lot of difficulty. My right foot was much better than it had been in many years. Having the extra length in my right leg also enabled me to walk much better, especially going uphill. My low back pain was not as bad when I walked a long distance. I now had the incentive to get back on my daily diet regiment. I had put on a good 10 to 15 pounds from May of 2020 until 2021. I wanted desperately to shed that weight.

Pamala and I enjoy walking together, though we walk in very different ways. I think about my pace and stride length and don't talk a lot. Pamala is known as a talker. She never meets a stranger. She can easily talk to everyone and remembers names and every detail of their lives. She has many friends because of her personality. She loves to be with people. Pamala likes to walk and talk or what I call, "stroll and talk." My competitive nature comes out and I'm focused on how fast I'm walking each mile and trying to do what I can to beat the time I walked the day before. Pamala doesn't care how fast we walk, though she walks faster than I am able to walk. If there is a home for sale and they are having an open house, she wants to go inside and see it. She wants to stop at garage sales. I want to complete the walk and set a new record time every walk. Nevertheless, we both look forward to our daily walk. When she can't walk with me, I miss her.

Just as I began feeling better and our routine returned to normal, I noticed my back pain flared again. My lower back worsened by the week. Dr. Brinker referred me back to Dr. Moore, but said it was not out of the norm for patients to experience pain as they stretched and used body parts that hadn't been used before the surgery. He said my body needed to adjust to walking a whole new way.

By late July 2021, I experienced much greater pain in my lower back and my legs felt heavy. I usually felt some lower back pain at the beginning of each walk, but the pain went away after the first half mile and then returned toward the end of our walk. Now, the back pain persisted throughout our walk. I had sharp pain and heaviness in both my legs. My entire leg felt encased in some type of weighted pants. During the night, I awoke with painful leg cramps. Nothing I tried stopped them and I worried they wouldn't go away. They lasted for at least 10 minutes, and as soon as I thought they were easing, they returned in full force.

I received regular injections in my back from the neck area down to the lower back for well over a decade. I have received every treatment the pain management doctors offered including nerve burns and steroid injections. The back injections gave me total relief for as long as a year, but over the last five years, I started getting back injections and nerve burns every six months. However, over the previous two years, what little relief I did get only lasted up to a month. During Covid, the injections were performed but the wait was much longer. Once I had the external fixator installed, I was not given any steroid injections because the injections slow bone growth. I got an injection shortly before the fixator was installed and got no relief. In January 2021, Dr. Brinker gave me permission to get an injection in my lower back. Because I was having such lower back pain, he felt we were far enough along that the steroid shot wouldn't have a negative effect on the bone growth. The injection gave me no relief. The pain management doctor did a second injection and nerve burn to give me some relief, but this did nothing to provide any relief to my back. The pain in the back of my legs limited how long I could stand and walk. I finally decided to contact Dr. Moore in early September 2021.

We love doing things with our grandchildren during the summer and things in our area were much more open in the summer of 2021 than they had been the previous year. We made up for lost time as best we could, but my leg and back pain prohibited me from doing much by the end of summer. I did my best to push myself, but our daily walks completely halted because of the pain. By the time I arrived at Dr. Moore's office, I struggled to walk from the car to his office. He reviewed past exams and said there were places in the thoracic region and the lumbar region that had previously shown degenerative arthritis and discs that were well worn. My symptoms required him to order an updated MRI immediately. He requested the imaging company make a CD containing all prior images of my back including the one that I had just completed. As I checked out, I asked for the disc and the nurse told me to take a seat and she would have it shortly. After about 30 minutes the nurse came out and apologized for taking so long to get the disc ready. She said over 1200 images of my back were downloaded. Although I knew I had a lot of MRIs performed of my back, I was amazed to learn there were 1200 images at this one imaging center!

Dr. Moore is a large man physically. His personality is as large as he is. He fills the room with his warm demeanor and outgoing personality. He is confident without being arrogant. Dr. Moore is quiet. He is very active in the Austin area and is the doctor for the Austin rodeo and many other large charitable events. He attended the University of Texas on an athletic scholarship in the 1960s. He has experienced several serious accidents and endured a lot of major surgeries himself. I believe this helped make him the compassionate man he is today. Even back in the 1980s when I first met him, I felt he had an easy bedside manner, and I could talk about whatever I was experiencing. He almost always spends the first 10 minutes asking about what is going on in my life and family. The visits start out with the feeling of a chat with a friend more than a doctor's appointment. After small talk, he usually cracks a quick joke or two before settling in to discuss what brought me into the office. For me, another big plus for any doctor is always being on time, which he is. I feel punctuality shows a physician's respect for their patients. If they are running a few minutes behind schedule from time to time is one thing, but there are some doctors I've visited who were always 45 to 60 minutes behind. Dr. Moore is busy. He takes his time with each patient, but somehow stays on schedule. Dr. Moore always sits down throughout the visit and doesn't stand until all my questions are answered, often continuing to talk even after stepping out into the hallway.

Chapter 24

SEVERE AGAIN!

Pamala went to my follow-up appointment in September. Instead of Dr. Moore's usual small talk and jokes, this visit went a bit differently. He walked into the exam room in a serious mode and handed Pamala and I each a printout of the MRI report. He looked at us with a look that let us know he was serious and said in a very matter of fact way, "I want you to read along with me as I point out several areas of the report." As Dr. Moore read aloud the three- page report of the MRI, we followed along and then he pointed out the word "severe," which was in bold black letters and all caps. He repeated the word "severe" several times. He looked up from the report and asked, "Do you see the word severe? I want to review this portion again because I want to be clear how serious this report is and what it means. The MRI report doesn't say you have areas where your back is bad, but this report says your back is in severe condition."

The imaging report used the word "severe" to describe multiple regions of my back. He then turned around to the computer in the exam room, pulled up the MRI images and showed us the areas of my spinal cord that had been listed as severe. Even to the untrained eye, I saw my spinal cord was completely collapsed flat at the L3, L4, L5 and S1 level. He pointed to one image and said it was a slice of my spinal cord that looked at the back as if someone was standing at my feet. If my back was a loaf of bread, it would be looking at an individual slice from the end. This image showed one very small white spot showing all the spinal fluid that was able to get beyond the L3 level. He said I needed to be referred immediately to a neurosurgeon at Houston Methodist Hospital in the Houston Medical Center.

For just a moment, we sat taking in what we heard. I asked the doctor if I had any other option besides back surgery and if he felt it necessary for me to go to Houston. I knew all the hospitals in the Houston Medical Center were some of the best hospitals in the world, but Austin is a great medical community that includes Seton Dell Hospital, the newest University of Texas Medical School. My spinal cord collapsed and the nerves at the lumbar level were in poor condition. Dr. Moore said I could opt out of the surgery, but eventually I would be permanently paralyzed from the waist down. Organs such as my bladder would be paralyzed as well. The nerves were in such severe condition that there would be no hope of the nerves regenerating once paralysis hit. He said, "you can schedule the surgery, or you need to get busy picking out a wheelchair you will spend the rest of your life in." He also deemed it necessary to travel to Houston for surgery by one of the best neurosurgeons in the United States, Dr. Robert Parrish at Houston Methodist Hospital. Many considered Dr. Parrish to be one of the top three neurosurgeons in the United States. Houston

Methodist was considered one of the best hospitals for this type of surgery.

Before we left the exam room, Dr. Moore went back through the MRI report one final time and noted the word "severe." He said time was of the essence and made it clear I would be paralyzed from the waist down before the end of the year if I didn't have the back surgery soon. The year's end was just a little over two months away. Dr. Moore also told us Dr. Parrish discussed retiring soon and he wanted to make sure Dr. Parrish performed the surgery.

My wife and I drove to Houston to see Dr. Robert Parrish in early November. We were thankful to see a highly recommended doctor and possibly get some relief for my back, but the dread of another surgery and the three-hour drive to Houston brought a very mixed set of emotions. We had just spent a year going back and forth to Houston for the external fixator, and now we were returning to stay in the same hotels and eat at the same restaurants. My legs grew worse daily during the two-week period between seeing Dr. Moore and Dr. Parrish. My legs felt heavier, and the pain was there 24 hours a day, 7 days a week.

Levi, my grandson who was four years old at that time, was going to be home for Halloween. Our neighborhood goes all out for every holiday. Families gather on each block and give away hot dogs or hamburgers and candy for the kids. Many families host multiple games for the kids to play.

Kids are everywhere. We looked forward to spending time with Levi because this was the first time to be home at Halloween. Levi was excited and looking forward to the food and games all day on October 31. He could hardly wait to go through our neighborhood. As it got later in the day, he could hardly be held back. About 5 p.m., we couldn't hold him back anymore, so we started down the street. When we rounded the first corner and had gone just blocks, we came to a house with tables filled with hamburgers and hot dogs, all kinds of kid's games, and candy to give away. The homeowners took down a section of their fence so the kids could easily get to the games. Several neighbors came together to provide food, games, riding toys, and lots of candy. Levi was having a blast and rode several toys. After about 15 minutes, he was ready to find the next house with more toys and treats. Sadly, I walked as far as I could go. My legs felt like they were encased in cement blocks and the back of my legs were on fire. I told Pamala to go on with Levi and I would return home where I would sit on the porch until they returned. I think at that point I realized just how bad my back had gotten because we had walked only five minutes from our home. My legs felt like they each weighed several hundred pounds, and it took everything I had to make it back home. I knew if I deteriorated this quickly, I needed surgery or I wouldn't be able to walk at all.

I was glad when Pamala and I drove to Houston in preparation for my appointment. We went through our old routine of eating breakfast at a place we loved there. We traveled from there on the same route we used in the past to get to the Medical Center. Houston traffic gradually returned as Covid lessened. What took us 30 minutes a year earlier, now took an hour. We left the hotel early Monday morning to be sure we arrived at the hospital on time. I was instructed to arrive an hour before my appointment for x-rays, then to go to Dr. Parrish's office.

Dr. Parrish, in his 70s, was a friendly surgeon with a long-distinguished career in neurosurgery. He took my case in part due to his respect for Dr. Moore. He said when Dr. Moore referred patients to him, they went to the top of his list. He respected Dr. Moore and knew patients had to be in serious condition if Dr. Moore referred them. Dr. Parrish reviewed the images taken that morning as well as the MRI images taken several weeks prior in Austin. He said I needed a laminectomy. I asked if there were any other options other than surgery. Dr. Parrish said the two options were to have the surgery or discuss the type of wheelchair in which I would want my paralyzed body to spend the rest of my life. Dr. Parrish said the nerves could regenerate if he operated now, but paralysis would prohibit the nerves from regenerating. The choice was obvious, though I dreaded the thought of another surgery, especially a back surgery. At this point, I had been through 85 major surgeries and had no idea how many day surgeries. I also spent a year dealing with the Illzarov external fixator surgery. My legs were deteriorating so fast that I knew we had to do something. Dr. Parrish reassured us that it shouldn't take more than a month's time and I would be back to walking daily and be glad we did the surgery.

Because the week of Thanksgiving was just a couple of weeks away, we couldn't schedule the surgery before November 30. Dr. Parrish ordered a full heart workup at Hermann Hospital, next door to Methodist Hospital. He referred me to his personal cardiologist for the testing since my surgery needed to be done in a short period of time. We returned a week later for a stress test and other cardio testing. I passed with no issues. We returned home and celebrated a great Thanksgiving with family. My legs got progressively worse each day. Finally, on Sunday November 28, we drove to Houston, had a good meal that evening, and prepared for the next couple of days.

After pre-testing Monday morning, we spent the rest of the day shopping in the Galleria area. I sat most of the day while my wife shopped. I was quickly getting to the point where I couldn't walk from the car to the stores. My legs were too heavy and the pain too great. We went to bed early Monday night because we had to be at the hospital by 6 the next morning. We drove to Houston Methodist on Tuesday, November 30 ready for surgery. It was still dark outside when we arrived at the surgical area around 6:15. Within minutes of walking into the surgery waiting area, I was taken back and quickly prepared for surgery. The IV was started, my vital signs taken, and my wife was allowed to go back with me. She hadn't been there long when Dr. Parrish arrived and said the surgery would take two hours and that I should be awake in recovery by noon. He said if I felt like going back to Austin that afternoon, he would release me. He said whatever I decided to do he would make it happen. I could either go home that day or stay the night and head back to Austin the next morning.

After falling asleep in the operating room, I woke up screaming in pain. My legs felt as if they were being crushed and the pain was unbearable. I don't remember a lot except I was in as much pain as I had ever been in during my 40 years following the accident. I went back to sleep after taking more medication. I was still in great pain when I woke up a second time. I wasn't thinking about going home at this time. My only thought was how long would this level of pain last. I screamed in pain as I was rolled to my hospital room. I opened my eyes to see an elevator filled with people. I did my best to not make any noise, but the pain was unbearable. In my room, I begged the staff to give me something that would put me to sleep. Pamala later told me that it took her a while to walk from the surgical waiting area to the tower where the hospital rooms were located. She heard me screaming when she stepped off the elevator onto the floor. Thankfully, medication kicked in and I fell back to sleep. I am not sure of the timeframe, but I remember waking up for a few minutes and still feeling like a 10 on the pain scale. I no longer screamed in pain, but I couldn't be still. The nursing staff ordered me to remain flat, but it was difficult to lie still while suffering excruciating pain. It felt like someone was stretching my leg muscles to extreme levels. As I opened my eyes, I saw my wife standing next to the bed. I was facing away from the doorway to the room when I heard a nurse behind me ask my wife a question I will not soon forget.

Has your husband been awake long enough for you to explain everything that has gone wrong?" the nurse asked.

My wife had not had time to tell me anything but was rubbing my arm to calm me. I glanced at the clock and saw it was 8:45 p.m. I had no sense of how long I had been out of surgery which ultimately took over eight hours. Dr. Parrish told Pamala he had never seen a spinal cord so damaged. He spent over six hours drilling away the bone because the bone had become four to five times thicker than the average bone. He feared I may have bone disease.

It was a long night. Every time I awakened, I was in extreme pain, and they would give me medication strong enough to put me back to sleep. The next morning, Dr. Parrish said he was in shock that I had been able to walk into his office. He drilled for hours before reaching my spinal cord. When he finally reached it, he found it was flattened and the dura or covering of the spinal cord and brain was worn to the width of a piece of paper. He first removed the pain pump because the catheter was in the way of where he needed to drill, but my spinal cord had leaked for some time from where the catheter went into my spinal cord. He repeated several times that he had not seen a spinal cord in as bad a shape as mine in almost

40 years of neurosurgery. He repaired at least five leaks, but my spinal cord still oozed spinal fluid in several additional areas. Dr. Parrish didn't understand how I could physically walk into the hospital that morning or even walk into his office three weeks before. Dr. Parrish felt he closed the places where the spinal cord leaked, but he felt it best for me to stay in the hospital for at least a week to 10 days.

I had to lie flat on my back for at least seven days to stop the leakage. The next few days were difficult. I could not raise my head. The pillow I was given was no more than two inches thick. I could move my arms and legs, but it felt suffocating. I would lay items such as my iPhone or iPad down and then search for them with my hands. I called the nursing staff to assist me in finding whatever I laid down. I felt so helpless and frustrated because I could not do it for myself. When Pamala returned home, I had to rely on the nurses for just about everything.

Pamala owns a small store in the downtown area of Dripping Springs called "Home Sweet Home." She sells home décor, antiques, and items such as locally made salsa and jams. The store is open Tuesday through Saturday from 10 a.m. until 5 p.m. Fridays and Saturdays are busy days with all the tourists who come through our area. As word spread through our friends and community, it was touching how quickly they all came together to assist my wife and I. Pamala brought enough clothes to stay for two days and needed to go home for more clothing. When my wife told my mother-in law, Elsie Hughes, we needed to go to Houston for this surgery, Elsie volunteered to keep the store open through Thursday of that week. Once word spread about my serious complications and my extended hospital stay, our friends and regular customers volunteered in the store to keep it open. Though Pamala had numerous friends fill in for her, she still needed to return home every few days to attend to certain details. My wife's friends, including many business owners in Dripping Springs, dropped by daily to say they would do everything in their power to keep the store going. Both of our sons, Danielle, and other family members volunteered to assist with the church and my wife's shop.

Pamala's shop boasts everything from sofas and armoires to candles and dish towels. She constantly restocks and restages the store. She is always going to her storage to get items to fill in the newly left holes when people pick up their furniture. She loves decorating and the shop is her dream job. Not only does she decorate the shop, but she is often hired by customers to assist them in decorating their homes. She has built a large and loyal clientele and has a steady stream of tourists who come through looking for a special piece they can take back home. Thankfully, her wonderful friends could stage and keep the shop looking attractive as normal. I knew Pamala needed to return home to keep things on track. I hate that she spends so much time with me at a doctor's visit or in a hospital room, but I am always sad to see her leave. Anytime she goes back home,

I'm count the days and hours until her return. I have peace when she is present. My greatest comfort is knowing she is sitting nearby.

My leg pain gradually improved over the first three days following the original surgery. Pain in the surgical site lessened in pain, but the constant lying flat on my back became very uncomfortable. Because Pamala was not there and I had to lie flat to feed myself, I constantly spilled food and liquids on me during each meal. I couldn't avoid it. I felt dirty after every meal. I changed hospital gowns five to six times a day after eating, brushing my teeth, or shaving. The patient staff cleaned me and changed my bedding several times a day.

I received clearance to roll on my side the second day after surgery but only for a few minutes at a time. I was told to log roll, a slow roll with legs and torso all rolling at the same time. I could not hold onto the side of the bed to pull myself in position but could push gently with one leg. I spent about five minutes on my side each hour and then rolled flat onto my back again. The thing I hated more than anything was the hourly check for a possible cerebrospinal fluid (CSF) leak. During each inspection of the bandage, nursing staff checked to see if any blood from the incision contained spinal fluid. After five days of this routine, Dr. Parrish ordered an MRI of my head and back to determine if there were any spinal fluid leaks.

Dr. Parrish said he would discuss letting me go home if the MRI came back without any signs of spinal leaks. He said the MRI showed no leakage, but he wasn't convinced that was the case. Because I had a slight headache and a ringing in my ears, Dr. Parrish believed there was still a leak somewhere or a high possibility that a leak could occur at any time. He said the dura or covering of the brain and spinal cord had been damaged for a long period of time, possibly dating back to my fall or maybe from previous back surgeries.

Eight days after my surgery, a physical therapist attempted to help me stand. She reminded me to move slowly. Just to sit on the side of the bed for a few minutes felt wonderful. There was no additional pain or ill effects, so she said I could attempt to get to my feet. As I began to stand, things felt fine at first. I tried to stand, but the pain in my legs was unbearable. I collapsed back onto the bed. The following morning, I made a second attempt to stand. I pushed through the pain and stood completely upright for a few minutes. It felt great to be out of bed on my feet, but the pain in my legs was indescribable. I quickly sat back down on the bed. The pain began to subside, and it got easier to stand. After another day or two, I could walk to the restroom in my hospital room and took my first shower since my surgery. Showers, shaving, and brushing my teeth are simple things, but they always make me feel better. I felt full of hope and excited that I could soon return home. Things improved to the point that by December 9, Dr. Parrish said I could go home the next day. There is something about sleeping in my own bed, being at home, and having my family around me, especially my grandkids, that relaxes me. It encourages me to work hard at getting back to my routine.

The morning of December 10, I ate breakfast and got dressed as my wife packed my belongings. In no time, the transport team arrived with a wheelchair to wheel me out of the hospital. I requested one final trip to the restroom. I was feeling fine. The pain in my legs dissipated and my headache improved. For the first time, I felt like everything was on track. I looked forward to settling back into a routine at home and hearing the sound of my grandkids playing. Doctors and nurses repeatedly told us to return to Methodist Hospital if we saw even one drop of fluid leak from the incision.

Chapter 25

SEVEN WEEKS OF SETBACKS AND DISCOURAGEMENT

The nurse and my wife tried to load our belongings on the cart provided by the hospital. I got out of bed and made my way to the restroom using my walker. As I stepped into the restroom, Pamala said, "You've got a large wet area on the back of your shirt." I blew it off and told her that I had washed my hair in the bathroom sink. I was sure it was just water that ran down from my hair onto my shirt. The nurse feared I had a spinal fluid leak and commanded that I get back in bed. She ordered me to lie flat on my back again until I saw the doctor. Fluid gushed down my back when she squeezed around the incision site. She confirmed it was a spinal leak and said I would not be going home. When the doctor examined my incision, he agreed it was a spinal fluid leak. He scheduled surgery for the next day.

This setback was beyond frustrating. I went from the high of being minutes away from leaving to the low of being back in bed on my back and preparing for surgery in less than 24 hours. I saw any setback as a challenge when I was younger. The "I'll show you" attitude immediately kicked in and I quickly bounced back. It now takes me days, if not weeks sometimes, to get in the right frame of mind.

Several of the neurological residents checked me for any number of issues, including the possibility of an infection or any stroke-like symptoms. The nursing staff declared it even more important than before that I stay on my back. I watched my wife unpack all the belongings she had loaded onto the cart. An array of emotions washed over me as I went from being discouraged and upset to being thankful that the leak happened while in the hospital. The worst feeling of all is that I felt I had let down my wife and everyone else. This forced my wife to spend more time with me in the hospital, to travel back and forth to Dripping Springs, and to worry about asking people to work in her shop.

I was most disappointed about letting our church down. I could not be there to shoulder the burden and the role of a pastor. Our church people love working in and around the church, and they gladly fill their roles, but I am paid to handle the daily pastoral tasks. The church took on extra expense for someone to speak in my place for an unknown number of services. Some in the church needed me to be strong and pray for them. I could not do anything because I was stuck in a hospital room for an undetermined period, even though the medical team was trying to get me home for Christmas. Some may think these are small concerns, or simply me feeling sorry for myself, but I am being transparent. I genuinely felt I let everyone down.

I owe a great debt for the many years my family and friends sacrificed on my part. They willingly give of themselves all because of an accident that happened in mere seconds 40 years ago. I'm not comfortable when someone "does a favor" for me. I have always been independent and wanted to do things for others. I served as the protector of my younger brother and sister. As a young person, I planned what we were going to do or where we would go. I didn't seek out this role, but it was something I was comfortable doing. I like to be the one who pulls things together for the group. I have also volunteered for various boards and charity groups. When my sons played baseball in high school, I was elected to be president of the high school baseball booster club. I didn't see it as a duty. I wanted to be involved. One of the more difficult things for me is letting others help me with simple tasks that I can't physically do anymore.

Both my wife and the nurse tried to console and encourage me. They didn't see me do anything to cause the leak. It was out of my control. I tried my best to follow the three basic rules they preached: no bending, no lifting, no twisting. The nursing staff said a gallon of milk weighed just under 10 pounds, and I was limited to lifting no more than that. I had been cautious and as careful as possible. Pamala placed anything she thought I may possibly need in the stand beside the bed. When taking a shower, I used the tools the hospital staff provided to help me reach my back and get in the shower. All of this was done to no avail.

Plans for the next day's surgery called for closing any leaks and installing a drain to help drain the spinal fluid from my back. Pamala scrolled through contacts on both our phones and asked everyone we knew to pray. As the evening wore on and surgical staff prepared me for surgery, I couldn't help but feel like I had hit rock bottom and failed everyone. Tears flowed down my cheeks as I sobbed. I hit one of my lowest emotional moments.

The next morning at 6:30, December 11, medical staff wheeled me to the pre-surgical preparation area. Thankfully, the staff had compassion for me, and allowed Pamala to stay with me because I was still very down emotionally. My wonderful wife is great at taking my mind off everything and does her best to keep me as calm as possible. She stayed with me until I was given enough mediation. I fell asleep even before they took me back to the operating room. Dr. Parrish previously told us the surgery should be no more than three to four hours. It turned into a 10-hour surgery due to numerous areas leaking spinal fluid. Dr. Parrish later reiterated that he had never seen a spinal cord in such poor condition. It had leaks from my neck to the base of the spinal cord. He took muscle out of my back, cut it into cubes, then placed the muscle inside my spinal cord to strengthen the dura. He expressed extreme concern about my condition and said I need to lie flat again. This time he didn't know how long.

On a positive note, the pain in my legs was completely gone when I awoke. For the first time in months, I felt no pain in either leg, and my back pain greatly improved. The drain placed in my back worked as it should, and I was flat as I could possibly be. This time, I was told not to turn on my side unless they rolled me over to check for a spinal leak. During surgery, doctors discovered the start of a staph infection growing inside the wound. This meant large doses of intravenous antibiotics. Dr. Parrish still pushed to get me home by Christmas.

When we first arrived at the hospital, I was asked to list my personal goals for life after surgery. It was difficult to even think about Christmas and the holiday season. The time from early November through the holidays is my favorite time of year. I couldn't think about the holidays without getting even more discouraged. I have always been able to muster mental strength and conjure up an "I-will- beat-this" attitude, but I felt totally defeated. I had been as still as possible. Although I had done what the doctors requested, the spinal leaks returned.

I was disrupting the holidays for my sons and their families, my siblings and their families, my mom, and my church. I guess from the outside looking in, this can be called a pity party, but I truly am concerned about what I put my family through over the years. Their lives are greatly disrupted by mine time and time again. This was far from the first time I had been in the hospital over the holiday period, but this was the first time that I was not in an Austin hospital over the holidays. On December 13, I felt well enough in body because I was sleeping for long periods at night for the first time in a long while. The leg pain was gone, and though my lower back was sore from the surgical pain, it wasn't that bad. My headaches came and went. Overall, I was doing much better physically, but I was a mental wreck. I was thankful for what God had done in taking away the awful leg pain and in blessing me with friends and family who came by to visit. I was also thankful for all those who assisted my wife with her store, but I found myself weeping and didn't always know why. The nurse from first spinal cord surgery continued to be one of my nurses. I asked her if leaving the hospital and resuming normal activities really could become a reality for me. She reassured me the leak was unavoidable and certainly nothing for which I was responsible. She repeatedly reassured me that I would leave the hospital before Christmas. She saw many people over the years with leaks like mine. The doctors found a way to get those patients' spinal leaks under control and they went on to live normal lives.

On the morning of December 14, just three days after my second surgery, I felt better physically than I had felt in months.

I started to get some hope back as the nursing staff and Dr. Parrish's staff restated that their goal was to still get us home by Christmas.

Pamala left the room about 11:30 to go pick up some lunch. By noon, I called the nurse and asked for pain medicine. My legs started aching in the same spot as they had in the past. The pain wasn't bad but was painful enough that I needed something to help give me relief. In less than 15 minutes, I called the nurse back to the room. I knew it wasn't anywhere near time for the next round of medication, but the pain worsened. She gave me a different medication. By the time she finished, my legs quickly reached the point that I couldn't handle the pain. The nurse stepped out of the room to contact my doctors. Before she returned, I started screaming due to the pain.

I was not overly surprised when my legs started to hurt because Dr. Parrish said the nerves had been trapped by the arthritic bone and the pain would return from time to time. He said the nerves would regain their ability to glide through the space he recreated, but it would take time and physical therapy. I don't remember Pamala returning from getting our lunch, but she again heard me screaming as soon as she stepped off the elevator. Pamala said I turned and twisted so much in the bed that I pulled the IV out of my arm. The nursing staff had trouble restarting the IV on a moving target! Pamala said I told the nursing staff to give me enough pain medication to put me to sleep even if it meant it would kill me. I didn't care what it took or the result as long as I was put out of my misery. The room filled with doctors and nurses all working to get the pain under control.

I'm glad God made our brains so that in these times there is a lapse of memory or at least the memory is somewhat foggy about the events. I don't know how to explain it or what takes place. I can't recall every detail from these extremely painful states. It is almost like a dream. God designed the brain so we are protected from what would be a horrible memory if we recalled each detail. Much like when I had my accident, I don't remember a lot of that day, but I have been told the details. I believe God designed us in such a way to protect us from these difficult times. I can't fully recall details of some of my traumatic events and feel God protects my mind. I went into a mental fog from the time I began to feel severe pain.

Finally, nurses started an IV in my left hand. Bruises and needle marks covered my arms and hands from the hours the nurses spent trying to start an IV the day prior. The IV didn't work properly, but it was effective enough to put me to sleep. It later stopped working completely. The excruciating leg pain lasted from around noon until 4:30 p.m. The pressure was so great that my head felt as if it were in a large vice. The room was filled with pain management doctors, residents, nurses, and a neurologist who gave me medications and did everything they could to control the pain during those four hours. After getting me to sleep, they quickly rushed me to imaging for a CT scan to check for a brain sag, a condition where too spinal fluid leakage causes the brain to sag. They also checked for signs of a possible stroke and for any fluid excess that would cause pressure on the brain. The scan returned with a normal result.

I don't remember the scan or much of the day. I slept the rest of the evening. My wife watched me go through this horrific event. I woke up later that night to the news that another surgery awaited me the next day, December 15. We both tried to rest that night, but it wasn't easy. I could tell my wife was concerned and under great stress.

This is when prayers of loved ones give us peace of mind and the ability to rest. Those who stop and really intercede on behalf of someone else in need are the most valuable friends. We all need those people who are willing to stand in the gap and to take the attacks of those they care for personally. When they hear or witness the enemy attacking their loved one's health, family, or finances, the prayer warriors go on the attack spiritually as if it were their own personal situation. We need those who help us fight the good fight of faith. I'm so thankful for pastors, fellow ministers, saints of God, and family members who bind together in prayer when I'm weak in body and weak in faith. While I may not be able to pray, I'm able to remain in the fight through their prayers. At times I try to pray, but the weight of everything I battle is difficult. I can't get my mind to focus well enough to get more than, "Oh God help me" out of my mouth. When my mind is in such turmoil that I struggle to put my thoughts and desires into prayer, I'm glad God knows what I need.

The church is important to me. Long after I walk out of a service, those who make up the church can fall on their knees in the middle of the night and wage spiritual warfare when I need the hand of God to intervene. There are those who love attending church for fellowship or maybe it's just what they grew up doing. Then, there are those who have developed a prayer life and are instant in season, and out of season are willing to drop to their knees in prayer. This is the real church. Those who go boldly before the throne of heaven for fellow members are the most valuable people in the local assembly. They can battle in prayer and are not afraid to bring down strongholds and wage war against hell itself. The Bible says the gates of hell shall not prevail against the church. This is not the church cowering in the corner as hell attacks, but this is an offensive position of the church going on the attack against the very gates of hell. Our God is not affected by distance. When I ask people to pray, they may be in other cities or even other countries, but their prayers are bound together as one.

Prayer is a great weapon of the church to battle against the enemy that comes to kill, steal, and destroy. Much like the neighborhood watch group that watches the homes and cars of those who live around us, the church body is a spiritual watch committee. We are not to gossip or talk about others. When I see the lives of those around me under attack, I immediately rally in prayer and wage war against physical, spiritual or mental attacks. We bind together and watch out for one another. If one person in my church is under attack, we are all under attack. If the enemy messes with someone in my church, he messes with all of us. That type of prayer and unity cannot be defeated by satan.

December 15, the day after the long day of difficult pain, proved to be another long day. The IV used to get me to sleep stopped working. Once I was taken to the pre-surgical area, the operating room nurses tried their best but couldn't get another

IV started. The anesthesiologist tried my legs and feet with no success and finally was able to get an IV started in my neck. It took the anesthesiologist at least eight attempts and well over an hour just to get an IV started. The anesthesiologist put me to sleep, and I did not wake up until nine or 10 hours later.

Dr. Parrish said the surgery went as well as could be expected, but it had been difficult. He found several additional spinal leaks that caused my sudden leg pain. He closed and replaced the drain, but my spinal cord remained in bad shape. The medical staff still believed I would go home before Christmas, but that seemed less and less likely.

I spent the next few days lying on my back and doing my best to not move unless it was necessary. I was afraid to move. If I moved even a little bit, I ended up in great pain with a spinal leak. My wife and I were worn out physically and emotionally drained. I cried over the smallest things. I lost hope that I would ever resume normal activity. Spinal leaks concerned me, but I feared that I would go from feeling fine to excruciating pain at any given time.

I was very low and greatly discouraged on Thursday morning when Christopher came to see me. I was glad to see him, but I wasn't really excited about him seeing me. I've always tried my best to be strong for my family, but that can only be carried out so far. Soon the only person you are fooling is yourself. I felt guilty that he drove all the way to Houston and then back to Austin just to see me. Christopher is always traveling as an evangelist. Instead of enjoying a few days at home, he drove over six hours roundtrip to see me. He talked a little bit about how amazed he was at the size of the hospital and the medical center. The small talk was good, but it was all I could do to hold back tears. He did his best to encourage me. I told him that I struggled to find the will to fight. I felt that I lost control when I couldn't remain calm during the severe pain. I think I am hiding my pain, but the only person I fool is usually myself. My wife gets extremely upset when I tell the doctor that all is well when it's not. She hears me complain about pain and knows about all my sleepless nights. She can't understand how I could be in such pain and not tell the doctor.

Chris kept telling me that I need to be honest with the doctors. He said that he was proud of how I handled all my obstacles with great class and dignity. He built me up and made me feel better. When he hugged me good-bye, I could no longer hold back the tears. I felt his love, but I also felt embarrassed and discouraged as if all hope was gone. I watched him leave and wept for a long time.

I also knew Pamala needed to leave the next day. It was difficult to know my biggest support would not be there. She left that Friday to take care of several issues at her store and get another change of clothing before returning Sunday, December 19. I watched the clock all morning. She couldn't arrive fast enough! I am completely torn when I know my wife must leave. I want her to be at home, relaxed, in our bed, and getting the rest I know she needs. At the same time, I can't wait until she walks back in the door. She loves to give gifts and do small things for me. She takes great care to make sure she gets something that I will like. She brought me two books and several puzzles, but I was too nervous to read anything or to focus enough to do a puzzle. Still, she tried, and I read the books after I got better.

That same day, pain slowly returned to my legs. It wasn't too bad at first but grew worse until late in the afternoon. The nurse asked that I roll over so she could check my bandages. I heard her loud gasp when I rolled over on my side.

I was blessed to have two ladies work as my nurses from the day I was moved onto that floor. They both worked 12-hour shifts. One worked the day shift, from 7 a.m. to 7 p.m. The other worked 7 p.m. until 7 a.m. Though there were other great nurses on that floor, I dreaded the days my regular nurses weren't there. They always contacted Pamala anytime something was amiss, and she wasn't at the hospital. They were both great at explaining my condition and the medical team's plans. Pamala and I had confidence in them and grew close to them. These two extremely competent nurses worked on the floor I was on for many years. This ICU floor is reserved for neuro-patients in serious condition. The large rooms gave them freedom to move around and offer the patients and family more room. These nurses had special training to handle serious patient issues. I will never forget their kindness and how caring they were in such a time of great need. I'm glad one of these two nurses was there Sunday, December 19.

I developed another spinal leak. Dr. Parrish scheduled another surgery for Monday, December

20. I was anxious and in a lot of pain. Pamala got

little sleep that night as she spent most of the night running her fingers through my hair, rubbing my face, arms, and hands, singing, and praying to get me through the night.

The surgery lasted eight to 10 hours. Dr. Parrish told me again about my spine's horrible condition. He placed a drain in my back to siphon the spinal fluid from my back into a large bag on the IV pole. There was also a device which measured how much spinal fluid drained from my spinal cord each hour. The damage to the spinal cord caused additional fluid to be produced by my body. The body produces spinal fluid much like saliva. My body was producing far more fluid than needed. To keep the proper amount of fluid in my spinal cord and brain, the nurses adjusted the device on the IV pole hourly. Too much fluid created pressure on the brain. Not enough fluid meant the brain would not have the needed fluid to keep it in place. Every hour, on the hour, the nurses stared at the bag and this device on the IV pole as they counted the number of drops of fluid flowing into the bag per hour. Normally, spinal fluid looks much like water, but my spinal fluid was a dark reddish color from all the surgery. The nurses constantly adjusted the amount of fluid drained from my spinal cord. At one point, the charge nurse told me the adjustment had been over corrected and they couldn't drain any fluid for a day because too much fluid drained in a short time. If too much fluid drains into the bag, the brain sags. If too much fluid builds up, extreme pressure is put on the brain. When the nurses stood by the IV pole for a long period, I got nervous thinking something was wrong. Sometimes they stood at the pole counting the drops that came out and then left only to return with another nurse and both stood staring at the IV pole. I took it as long as I could then said, "Okay, you've got to tell me something! You can't just stand there!" Usually it was something simple, but on several occasions, they called a resident because the fluid built up too rapidly. Pamala stared at the bag wondering what it was, but she did not want to ask. Finally, I said, "Just don't mess with that bag. It's my brain fluid." She tried not to show any concern, but she couldn't hide what she was feeling. I moved from my original room to be near others with a similar drain. Only certain nurses could handle patients with this type of drain. Moving all the things from one room to another was a chore and we didn't have the great view we'd had before, but these were small issues. At this point, our main concern was getting the drainage stopped.

I had another 10-hour surgery Tuesday, December

21. The resident who came felt they stopped the current leaks, but the dura was paper thin, the spinal cord continued to ooze fluid in various areas, and a leak could form at any time.

Spinal fluid soaked my bed later that evening. It was as if a water hose had been turned on inside my back. The nurses placed pads under my back, but I was leaking fluid at such a rate that the sheets would be soaked in spinal fluid every few minutes. The nurses feared this would cause stroke-like symptoms.

Residents came into my room several times an hour. Dr. Parrish quickly put together a team of doctors to assist him the following morning for the third straight day of surgery. The team included a general surgeon, another neurosurgeon, and a plastic surgeon. They came up with a plan to at least slow the spinal leaks.

Dr. Parrish and his team of surgeons planned to install a lumbar peritoneal shunt so that if there was any spinal fluid that leaked after the surgery, it would drain through the shunt. He handpicked the team consisting of general surgeons, cardiovascular surgeons, plastic surgeons, and several other neurosurgeons. He considered them to be the best in their fields at Houston Methodist. Dr. Parrish said they would spend the day working in relay fashion to repair my spinal cord, stop the leaks as much as they possibly could, and install a new drain as well as a shunt, which would allow the spinal fluid to drain into my bladder. Each surgeon came by that evening to explain what they would be doing. The words of Dr. Faraji, one of the neurosurgeons, stood out more than anything I heard that evening.

Dr. Faraji, a caring and compassionate man, chose not to speak about surgery details. He told the medical team in a pre-surgery meeting that he wanted to tell me there was hope at the conclusion of my surgery. There hasn't been a day since that I haven't thought of that statement. I needed hope more than anything. I had lost hope! Every time it seemed we would be released from the hospital, doctors would detect another leak. Hope diminished before making it to the finish line. I stopped allowing myself to hope. I reached down for something I couldn't put a name on, and I couldn't find it. That something was hope. I can't say I fell asleep that night and rested peacefully, but I can say I found the hope for which I yearned.

Doctors performed my 92nd major surgery, the longest of them all, the next morning, December 23. By the time I reached the pre-op area, I was practically bouncing off the bed with nerves. The anesthesiologist put me to sleep as quickly as he could. This would be the longest period I was ever under anesthesia. The general surgeon was delayed because of issues with inserting the central line. Each doctor after him took three to four hours to do what they were scheduled to do. Since it was just 2 days before Christmas, everyone in the post operative area wore some type of holiday hat or sweater. Some even had on other types of decorative holiday jewelry.

When I woke up from surgery, I thought I was at an underwater ski lodge and we were all floating around under water. I couldn't figure out why a ski lodge was underwater and wondered why in the world I was there. I finally came around and realized I was in the recovery room. When I was asked if I knew where I was, I was only able to answer because I heard another man answer the same question. Thankfully, his answer came at the right time or I might have answered that I was at an underwater ski lodge looking for my family!

Pamala waited all day in the waiting room, fearful of leaving and something happening or not being able to speak with each surgeon when they finished. That is how wonderful my wife is! When I arrived back at my room, I was still somewhat confused about the time of day because the surgery had taken so long. I left the hospital room around 6:30 a.m. and arrived back at my room late that night. Dr. Parrish said the surgery had gone well. The plastic surgeons and Dr. Faraji each played an important role in getting the leaks repaired and installing a new drain. Spinal fluid still leaked, but now it was draining into the shunt which led to my bladder. Dr. Faraji reassured me that I would be going home soon.

For the first time in a month there was fresh hope. I wouldn't let myself get too excited because I was fearful something would happen. I couldn't sleep for two nights because I feared that movement would cause another leak or pull something loose. The last thing I wanted to do was mess something up. The charge nurse said I had to eat right and get plenty of rest to heal. I told her about my fear of moving. I was as still as I could possibly be, but the pain in my lower back caused me to shift. Each time I adjusted my position, I held my breath so that there wouldn't be a leak. After a few days, the spinal fluid draining into the bag went from an orange color to clear for the first time. The nursing staff said that was the normal appearance of spinal fluid and a good sign of improvement.

Christmas came and went without much fanfare. For the first time in my life, I didn't think much about Christmas Day. My wife loves to give gifts. I was fearful she would bring me a Christmas present, and I wouldn't have anything for her. I enjoy Christmas shopping for her though it isn't always easy to find the perfect gift. Thankfully, she didn't put me in that position. This would be the first Christmas in 40 years of marriage that my wife and I didn't exchange Christmas presents on Christmas Day. There had been difficult Christmases where money was tight or I was in the hospital, but we still found a gift for one another. For the first half of our marriage, we usually spent Christmas on the road, traveling to see her family and my extended family, but on Christmas Day, we found time to exchange at least something small. Having family five hours away meant most years we celebrated Christmas a few days early and then spent the next several days traveling to see our families. This year, Pamala had been too busy driving back and forth to Houston to shop. While I know many shop for all their Christmas presents online, that just isn't how either of us prefer to shop for each other. I personally want to touch it. I want to walk in the shops and through the malls until I see that thing that grabs me and says, "Here I am, buy me." This Christmas we were just happy we weren't in surgery.

Things started looking up when 48 hours passed without surgery. Over the next week, the hope that Dr. Faraji wanted for me began to grow. I've thought about the importance of bringing hope to others ever since he made that statement. Hope helped me fight for my health, even though I had lots of anxiety.

On December 31, 2021, I was moved to another area for physical therapy and long-term rehabilitation. The therapist wanted me to list my most important goals. I asked if there were any limitations to these goals. The therapist said that the only limitations would be the limitations I put on myself. She said I could potentially do whatever I fought hard enough to do. I quickly put together a list that may seem simple to the average person, but all of these goals seemed impossible just a week before. This was a list of things I took for granted just a few months back but were now highly important for me to achieve.

My grandsons, Gentry and Levi, both love playing baseball. I wanted to coach them like I had once coached their fathers. One of my goals was to coach my grandsons' baseball teams. My two grandsons also love riding roller coasters. Number two on the list was to ride roller coasters with them. I had my hope back and my fight back. The list grew fast. When you have hope and are willing to fight for something, your mind has no limitations. I wanted to get back to walking three to five miles every day with my wife. I wanted to mow my own yard and go swimming with my grandchildren. I wanted to DO! I wanted to GO!

After listing my future goals, the therapist assisted me in standing and then in walking with the aid of a walker. The therapist made sure I knew and used the proper techniques to rise up from lying down and doing small things such as brushing my teeth, getting in and out of the restroom, or sitting up and eating. It was evident to the therapist I had already been through a lot of physical therapy because I already knew many of these techniques.

The rehabilitation area featured a restored 1970s Ford automobile. The doors had ropes and pulleys for wheelchair-bound patients to learn how to get in and out of the car. The also had a full kitchen with a refrigerator and a washer/dryer for patients to learn how to do the daily household tasks. The usual ramps and stairs were in the rehabilitation area. It seemed as if I had climbed those millions of times after surgery to prove I knew how to use crutches or walkers. There were all types of tools and gadgets to aid in picking up items from the floor or to use in the shower to eliminate the need to bend, twist, or lift while bathing. I saw young and old alike trying to restart their lives after a debilitating neurological injury or disease. As usual, there were some whose condition weren't all that bad, but they felt obligated to tell everyone their problems in detail. Those in serious condition rarely complained.

I visited the rehab room three times a day; twice for physical therapy and once for occupational therapy. The occupational therapist was a young lady in her early 30s who loved to talk about her relationship with her father. She was quick to laugh but a stickler for following the rules. My physical therapist was from Brazil. She had a heavy accent that was hard to understand at times. She was well qualified and adapted for her job. She gave me many small tidbits of helpful advice. She was also a stickler for following the smallest rules and quickly pointed out when you weren't doing something just right.

After the first few days, the therapist scheduled me for a timed walk. I walked down the hallway while the therapist walked behind me pushing a wheelchair with one hand and holding a stopwatch in the other. Physical therapy gets old quickly for me before I am ready for something different. My wife tried her best to help me pass the time. She pushed me in the evenings in a wheelchair and showed me areas of the hospital I hadn't seen before. I felt better and began to regain strength in my legs. I was unstable when standing, especially if I stepped to the side or backwards. When walking with the aid of a walker, I had to be careful not to trip when changing from one type of flooring to another. The longer I stood, the worse my balance became. Though I hated to admit it, I needed the walker. The occupational therapist used a lot of games to help me with my balance. We used the kitchen to learn how to get items out of the cabinet without reaching or stretching. She taught me how to use a reaching device. I wasn't allowed to pour milk because the carton weighed more than my 10-pound limitation, but there were a lot of small tasks I performed without twisting or bending.

Every few days, the therapist timed how quickly I walked a predetermined in the hallway. I improved each time. Assigned tasks seemed to get easier each day, building my confidence as I conquered each new challenge. I knew I was improving when the therapist corrected me for going too fast down one of the long hallways. The long corridor had a gradual rise at one end and then turned a corner as the hallway went up a floor level. I got to where I could climb the rise with a quicker pace.

The therapist said I could not go to the restroom or leave the room without my wheelchair or a therapist. I chose not to abide by that rule. I wanted to walk as much as possible to build my strength and get home sooner. I wanted to prove to the doctors that I could walk, but even more so, I wanted to prove to myself I didn't need a wheelchair. I took every opportunity to make myself stand. I stood while shaving and brushing my teeth. I snuck out of the room late at night when nurses were fewer in number and busy somewhere at the other end of the long hallway. The first few times, a nurse caught me without my wheelchair. I apologized and went back to my room without an argument. The nurses stopped taking my excuses. Finally, my nurse said they were putting an alarm on my bed that would go off if I got out of bed. They would know when I got out of bed without permission or without a nearby staff member.

Chapter 26

FINDING PURPOSE

I felt the "old me" quickly returning. I had my fight back and I was ready to take on whatever I needed to improve. Call it stubbornness, hardheadedness, or what my wife calls not being smart. Whatever it may be, it caused me to rise time and again when the doctors declared no hope. That part of the human spirit that causes one to fight for life is real. Viktor Frankl's book, *Man's Search for Meaning,* chronicles his time as a prisoner of war in Nazi concentration camps during World War II. Frankl tells how his viewpoint changed from first entering the camps and watching people around him die of starvation or at the hands of the camp guards. One of the things that helped him endure was his ability to imagine how he wanted his life to be when he got out. He built on that image in his mind each day. One of my favorite quotes from Frankl is, "Life is never made unbearable by circumstances, but only by lack of meaning and purpose." Without God's help, I would not have come through the many difficult times in my life and certainly could have never made it through the seven weeks at Houston Methodist.

I know God has blessed me far more than I will ever deserve, but I believe God wants us to do our part. I must look around and see all of God's many blessings that include my great wife, wonderful children, grandchildren, siblings, and extended family. They are my purpose to rise when I fall.

God created man so that he could face great trials and come out on the other side, if he has purpose. My grandchildren enjoy the time I spend with them. My wife needs me to enjoy life with her. I recently walked into an office where a young man who was born with a debilitating disease worked at the reception desk. He couldn't use his arms but blew into a tube to assist him in moving his wheelchair and typing on the computer. I can't imagine going through what this man has gone through, but he had a purpose and chose to not live his life stuck at home. He worked at improving himself so he could live a full life. No matter what we face, I believe we can put it in God's hands and ask God to give us a greater will, power, and the fortitude to say, "I will not allow this circumstance to defeat me!"

My dad and my grandfather cried if you told them that you loved them or when something special took place. I followed in their steps and can quickly to be moved to tears. I'm more likely to cry if my grandkids brag about me than over any great sadness. During my time at Houston Methodist, however, I found myself crying uncontrollably at times and I wasn't always sure why. I then realized that I stopped feeling a purpose for my life. When there was no purpose, there was no hope, and when there was no hope, there was no fight. Hiding from the world will never be the solution. There are people with real problems and very real challenges in our world. I have been with those whose spouse walked out and those given a devasting doctor's report. No doubt they faced great hurt and deep pain. Even the death of a spouse or loved one can be overcome when we find our purpose.

We are part of God's plan, and He has a purpose for each of us. Hospital volunteers who appeared to be in their late 70s or even early 80s pushed me in a wheelchair upon entering the hospital. I felt awkward when small-framed ladies who probably weighed less than 100 pounds pushed me, even though I was in pain. It just didn't seem right that someone I outweighed by 90 to 100 pounds and much older to push me. When I realized that was their purpose, I stopped making a fuss. They volunteered for that duty. They didn't have to be there. They weren't paid to be there. They volunteered because they wanted purpose. It gave them a reason to get up every morning. It gave them hope!

The physical therapist at Houston Methodist said she could tell I was a fighter and my attitude helped me overcome challenges in my life. Both the physical therapist and the occupational therapist corrected me daily for doing too much too fast, but that drive helps me overcome.

I have been caught sneaking out of the hospital over the years because I was tired of the hospital food and wanted something else to eat. One night, I went for a walk outside the hospital around 9 p.m. The front doors were locked as I was walking. When I returned and knocked on the glass door, the security guard told me I had to go to the emergency room to enter since it was so late. Once I showed him my armband and he saw that I was a patient, he opened the door. That refusal to just lie in a hospital bed or in bed at home is what has helped bring me out. Having a goal to achieve today and then anticipating how I will beat that goal tomorrow aids in fighting against the challenges I've faced.

When you have purpose, it is amazing how inventive you are. We had a kid's tic-tac-toe bean bag game with a plastic stand.

The Xs and Os were on individual plastic blocks that spun when hit with a bean bag. I tied a string to the bean bags and threw them at the Xs and Os, then dragged the bean bags back to me with the string.

When I spent a long period in the hospital and had to be in a wheelchair, I determined to learn how to pop a wheelie. I timed myself as I raced around the floor. After taking a break, I attempted to beat my previous lap time. Boredom and a desire to do more than wallow in self-pity sparks creativity. At times, this creativity got me in trouble or caused setbacks, but it has been worth it in the long term because I can do things that I was told I would not do.

I've received a scolding from nurses for sneaking out of the hospital or doing something in a wheelchair that caused them to instantly panic. I fell more than once because while testing how far I could spring ahead using my crutches. Challenging myself and adding a little fun helps me through the tough times,

I suffered from painful mouth sores brought on by the intubation tube inserted during each surgery. I could not physically brush my teeth for several days at a time. The sores caused a lot of pain even when I wasn't eating. Pamala went home for a few days, so I asked the occupational therapist to walk with me to Walgreens in the hospital to purchase some type of mouthwash, hoping it would help. The therapist got the clearance and found another to go with us. After walking part of the way, I sat down in the wheelchair while the occupational therapist carried my walker. I asked if I could roll myself in the wheelchair to help strengthen my arms. When walking with my wife, I learned there was a steep downhill area around the hallway corner. As we neared that area, the therapist started to step over to make sure I made it safely down the hill. I didn't wait for her. I gave both wheels a big shove and then raised my hands like someone on a roller coaster. The wheelchair rolled swiftly down the hill, and I went flying down the hallway while my occupational therapist ran behind me screaming, "STOP!" I safely reached a level area and the wheelchair came to a rest.

The therapist quickly caught up to me and demanded that I "NEVER, EVER, do anything like that again." She lectured on the potential danger of turning over or running into a wall. That event was childish, but it made me feel alive again. I understood the therapist was responsible for me, but taking risks makes life fun. As we completed our trip to Walgreens, I realized I was quickly becoming my old self. I was regaining my purpose and my hope. Just a couple of weeks before, I had no hope, no purpose, and no fight. I had just raced downhill in a wheelchair and felt a rush that I hadn't felt in weeks!

When Pamala returned to the hospital, I felt much better and ready to get out of the room for more than physical therapy. I asked the therapist and charge nurse if we could take an extended walk. Once the nurse agreed, I then had to get the therapist to agree. I knew she was still upset about my wheelchair stunt. I also knew both Pamala and the therapist were strict rule followers so I had to promise that I would be on my best behavior. The therapist agreed, but only if we took the wheelchair because I would need to ride if we went very far. The therapist and Pamala talked about what rules I had to follow. It felt good to explore and meander down the hallway for the first time in over five weeks. I didn't make it far walking and I willingly collapsed in the wheelchair. I pushed myself in the wheelchair until my strength gave out and then let Pamala push me. I still had no desire to go back to my room. We explored the many areas Pamala discovered during our time there. The long hallways that go on for blocks have many different stores which we visited. For the first time in over a month, I felt human. I developed cabin fever as I approached six weeks in the hospital. I yearned to get out of the hospital but guarded my hopes. I wanted to get back to my routine and my family.

A scan of my abdomen revealed the shunt had come undone at some point. Doctors scheduled a simple procedure to lengthen the tube to the shunt and put it back in place. He said they would possibly remove the drain as well.

After two weeks of physical and occupational therapy, the therapists had a hard time coming up with things that challenged me. I'm thankful for the team that worked with me and helped me literally get back on my feet. On the last day of physical therapy, I walked the hall one last time as the therapist timed me. She was shocked at how fast I walked the nearly 1000 steps down the hallway as she followed pushing a wheelchair. I not only made the walk in a very fast time but did so without falling back into the wheelchair when I finished the walk. I cut my time almost in half in just two weeks and felt I could have gone much farther. I went from walking well over three miles with my wife a few months prior to walking just 1,000 steps, but I was happy. I felt confident my daily walks with my wife would resume.

I said good-bye to both therapists who had spent so much time with me over the past two weeks. I owed them a great debt because they encouraged and helped me attain my physical goals. That accomplishment causes a patient to feel a close bond with therapists. They helped improve my physical stamina and ability. Even more importantly, they gave me the mental strength and hope to build up to whatever distance I desired. I will always be appreciative for all those over the years who spent time to get me put back together both mentally and physically. I know the physicians are paid well for doing their jobs, but there are those that go through the motions, and there are also those who genuinely care for their patients. There are nurses that have become so hardened to what they've seen that it has become just a job. Then, there are those who have worked years in the medical profession yet have tears in their eyes as they work with me during very difficult times. They truly care for their patients.

My advice to those with chronic medical conditions is to take charge of your medical journey. Whether you are dealing with physicians, therapists, nursing staff or pharmacists, it is your body, your money, and your time. You must take charge of making sure you know as much about your care plan as possible. You must make sure you are more than a chart number to all those who are treating you. I also advise:

- Contacting the patient advocate with concerns which haven't been resolved. Advocates can make magic happen! They are truly on the patient's team. Every hospital and most doctors' offices have one. They helped me time and time again.

- Always sign a medical power of attorney anytime you go into the hospital. I've forgotten my medical power of attorney at home and asked the nurse for a copy prior to surgery. Since the form needs to be witnessed by non-medical personnel or family members, I have gone around the waiting area and asked complete strangers to witness the form. When I explained I just needed a signature to show that I had completed the form, I've never been turned down. If something happens, my spouse has the power of attorney to transfer me to another hospital or request another doctor. She holds the same power I do to make medical decisions. During Covid, several families wanted to transfer loved ones from one facility to another, but they couldn't because they didn't have a signed medical power of attorney. It is a simple form you can get online. A local hospital can provide you with the short 2- page form.

- Always keep in mind that you are in charge of your care! The best doctors have no problem with you getting second or third opinions. They are confident enough in their abilities that they are glad you get further opinions. Doctors who are less sure of themselves will sometimes get frustrated when you want more than one opinion. I may feel a doctor is great at his job but our personalities are not compatible and I will continue searching for a doctor who is not only capable, but one who takes time to hear me out and listen to what I am saying. If a doctor is too busy to hear me out, I will not go back. They may be highly recommended and be more than qualified, but if I can't talk to them and tell them what I feel, then I move on to another doctor. There are many great doctors who will listen. They will care for you and will oversee your care.

- Do your research and check your bill. How we do medical insurance in America has led us not to investigate the cost of our treatment. We know what our co-pay is, but we don't know what one facility charges for an x-ray versus another facility. This has led to higher medical costs. We don't know what we pay.

- If you are not satisfied with how you are treated, go elsewhere. If the physician is always late, I find someone that is aware that I also have things I need to do, and they need to be mindful of my time as well as theirs. I have seen highly capable doctors who were way behind in their schedule and were rude when they came in. They rushed me when I tried to ask questions and when the visit was over, I let them know I appreciated their time, but I would in no way let someone with their attitude treat me during what would be a mentally difficult time in my life. I've had more than one nurse who was rude while I was in the hospital, and I called the patient advocate and let them know I did not want the nurse back in my room. I try to do it as politely as possible, and I give the advocate specifics but the advocate will see to it that you are not given that nurse again. Many years ago, I had a major surgery and was in a lot of pain after surgery. The nurse who came into my room that night decided I didn't need the amount of pain medication that had been ordered by the surgeon. She felt the surgery wasn't as painful as the surgeon said it was and that I should be able to endure the pain with simple Tylenol. I was in a great deal of pain, just as the surgeon had told me I would be prior to the surgery. He said it would be an extremely painful surgery and ordered extra pain medication that was to be overseen by a pain medicine physician. My wife, who had the medical power of attorney, told the patient advocate what was going on. The patient advocate spoke to the C.E.O. of the hospital. She also spoke to the charge nurse, the floor nurse, and the pain management doctor. That nurse was not my nurse for the rest of my stay in the hospital. The CEO of the hospital even came to my room and apologized for the nurse withholding pain medication the surgeon ordered.

Taking charge of your care plan doesn't mean you think you know more than those trained in the medical field. We must lean on them to treat us and to care for us. I always tell doctors, "I haven't been to medical school. I am leaning on you to make the right decision." Having a good relationship with the doctor is important. You only have one body. It is more important than your car or home. Those can be replaced but you have been given only one body. Don't feel like you can't speak up. I have told numerous doctors, "One of us is paying, and one is getting paid. The one paying is not happy with the one getting paid."

I have as many as two to three medical appointments a week. Sometimes working them into my schedule is difficult. I've had almost all my physicians for more than a decade and have worked hard to establish a relationship with them. Most were recommended by another doctor. When I find a knowledgeable physician who fits my personality, I know I will be at ease when I see them. This allows me to be more comfortable in detailing what I am experiencing. I have a few surgeons who I am not sure I would want to go out to dinner with because our personalities are very different, but they are good at what they do and care for their patients, so I am at ease in telling them what I am going through. They take time to listen and hear me out. This is of the utmost importance when dealing with chronic health issues.

After two weeks of rehabilitation, I was taken back to one of the neurology floors and prepped for surgery the following day, January 11. This time, the surgery was just a few hours long. My wife was shocked when Dr. Parrish walked out so quickly and announced he had completed surgery. The drain wasn't removed until just an hour or so before we left the hospital. It was good to have it removed. The infection improved, but there was swelling in my lower back because the spinal fluid was still leaking more than the shunt could handle. Nevertheless, the group of doctors who performed the last major surgery felt I was able to go home. They instructed me to remain flat the first few weeks, and then slowly and gradually work my way up to walking two miles per day. I finally took the long-awaited ride down to where our car was waiting. I planned on lying down in the back seat, but I was ready to see the world. I had been stuck in a hospital for seven weeks and was ready for something other than the four walls of a hospital room. The hospital gave us pillows to use for my back while sitting and I made the ride home without too much difficulty. Dr. Parrish retired a week after I left the hospital. I was his final major challenge. He turned my care over to Dr. Faraji who has proven himself to be intelligent and caring.

We returned to the hospital two weeks after my release to visit Dr. Faraji and the plastic surgeon for a follow-up. They were concerned about the amount of swelling in my lower back. Normally, they would go back into my spinal cord and attempt to stop the leaks, but there were too many things that could go wrong. They feared if they made a large incision, the fluid may leak from the incision and give a pathway for infection to track to my brain. The surgeons had no desire to do any surgery or even tests that would puncture my spinal cord.

Chapter 27

WHAT'S NEXT?

As I write this, several months after returning home, there have been several major improvements, several areas of concerns also remain. Pamala and I are accustomed to completing one surgery only to move to the next surgery. What is more frustrating than moving to the next surgery is when we are told there is no sure way to move forward. Doctors have told me I am one of their more troubling cases. My headaches increased and I experience them almost immediately after getting out of bed each morning. The headaches come and go throughout the day and they rage by the end of the day if I've been up a long time. A laundry list of things needs addressed. Both of my hands need surgery due to severe arthritis. My right shoulder needs surgery for a torn rotator cuff. The broken hardware in my right foot needs attention. Several areas in my back that need to be fused or I need a laminectomy. Due to the continued leaks, doctors will not do the back surgeries unless it becomes an emergency.

There is a possibility the hardware in my right foot can't be removed, but the orthopedic surgeon said he must attempt to fuse the joints again in the foot that have a non-union. This non-union is due to the broken hardware as well as the brittle bone from the many surgeries and damage from the accident. I have arthritis in both feet and there are several areas which need surgical intervention.

By early April 2022, just a little under two and half months after my release, my wife and I walked most of our old route. We now walk 3.3 miles each afternoon. It took 90 minutes the first time I walked that distance. That is an embarrassing pace of a mile every 30 minutes. I once walked it at nearly half that time, but it felt so good to complete that distance.

I've had several appointments with other doctors for anemia and other areas of concern found in my blood work. We've addressed most with medication and have seen improvements. The chief concern is the continued spinal leaks and the constant oozing of fluid. We hoped the swelling in my back would go down as the leaks slowed, but the leaks have remained consistent. I started physical therapy twice a week in February and have improved my balance. Thankfully, I stopped using a walker by late March. The doctors told me they fear I will have "stroke-like symptoms" due to either fluid buildup in my head or a lack of fluid that would cause my brain to settle to the bottom of my skull.

In mid-April, Dr. Faraji ordered a CT-scan that showed no major build-up of fluid in my brain, but the leak caused the swelling in my low back to grow larger than it was when I got out of the hospital. Dr. Faraji has told me on several occasions that he is concerned about my health in the long term, and may be forced to do exploratory surgery in an attempt to close the larger leaks. The neurosurgeon wants to fuse my F5-S1 joint but is hesitant to do that for several more months. He will decide in the coming weeks and months what direction to go.

Chapter 28

HOPE AND FAITH RESTORED!

My hope is renewed, and my faith is increased to new heights because God brought me through a situation that I couldn't navigate myself. I know He is on the throne and in charge. I have faith that God loves me, cares for me, and sees exactly what I face each day and each night. I feel like the Psalmist who wrote these words in Psalm 73:26: *"My flesh and my heart fail; But God is the strength of my heart and my portion forever."* (NKJV).

Isaiah 40:31 is an often-quoted passage. We are told there are those who will renew their strength. Some will soar like eagles. Some will run and not faint. This is a promise for those who WAIT upon the LORD. Several Bible versions use the phrase, "they that hope upon the Lord." If I trust and wait on the God of glory, I will build hope in Him. When times seem the darkest, I can rest assured that He will come through for me. The only way I will ever renew my strength, soar like an eagle, and run and not faint is keeping my hope in Him.

My hope isn't always in a good doctor's report, education, finances, or the things of this life. Everything and everybody has disappointed me at some time. I love my family, but even they have disappointed me, and I've disappointed them. I've seen people put their hope in a job, only for that company to be sold to another company and they lose what they thought they had. I've been surprised on many occasions by a bad doctor's report.

My hope must remain in the One who will enable me to run and renew my strength. He knows there will be times when I will lose my strength. When my hope is in God, I can grab hold of Him and allow His spirit to lift me to lofty heights.

We have a lot of hawks in our area, and I enjoy watching them soar. It seems as if they can go forever without flapping their wings by catching the wind that comes out of a canyon. They soar higher and higher without a lot of effort, but they must ride the wind. God's spirit can lift you from the darkest hour in your life and help you soar when you feel forever grounded and hopeless. When you catch His spirit and put your faith and trust in Him, He will help you rise above the problems and issues and give you reason to really live. His hope is beyond this life, but in a life where there is no pain. I love this life because I enjoy my family. There is nothing like having my grandchildren in the living room at night after they've all had baths and are getting in the final few minutes of play time before they go to sleep. They put out pillows in our living room and use the hallway as if it is a runway. They will run with the skateboard and crash into the pillows. Their laughter is as good as life gets.

I grow older with each passing day, and one day I will leave this life. It doesn't end there because there is a hope far greater than anything this life holds. One

day, I will be limping along and the next step will be in the land where the lamb lies down by the lion, where there is no sorrow, no pain, no suffering, and no death, and I will never limp again! I will never stay in a hospital again. There will be no sickness and no need for IVs. There will be no blood draws, which means there will be no negative lab reports. One of the greatest things is that I will never hurt again physically or mentally. I wake up every night, because of pain somewhere in my body. When I get up each day, I know it will take 30 to 45 minutes to loosen my joints, but that is only temporary. I am thankful that I have a hope that goes beyond this life.

On those days I am in pain or the doctor's reports all seem to be coming back negative, I can still soar like an eagle. I can walk and not faint. On the days my arthritis causes me to ache and I walk slower than usual, I know that it is only temporary. When life comes crashing in and I can barely walk, much less run, I know I can make it if I focus on God who overcame death, hell, and the grave. I can overcome because He overcame. When chronic pain begins to wear on me, I remind myself that this is only temporary. Soon I will have a new body. I can run this race with hope because I don't have to lean on my own strength, my wisdom or understanding. I can lean on Him. He will enable me to run and not grow weary. He carries me.

Chapter 29

AFTER THE RESURRECTION, THERE'S HOPE!

The first day of the crucifixion meant death. The third day meant resurrection. On the second day, He went into hell and took back the keys of death, hell, and the grave from satan. The second day was a day the Jesus' followers awoke thinking about the loss from the previous day. They saw Jesus led away to the halls of Pilate from the garden. They watched as He was beaten and His beard plucked from his face. They watched as the crowd roared, "give us Barabbas," and they watched Jesus beaten until His body was almost torn in two. They watched Him as He was hung on a cross. They watched Him take His final breath, was laid in a tomb, and the stone rolled over the doorway of the tomb. When they woke on the second day, it seemed all hope was gone and all the miracles had ended.

Jesus found the disciples had gone back to the fishermen they once had been. They lost all hope. We have the advantage of hindsight. We have read the Word of God and know that He arose on the third day. All the disciples had was the prophetic word of the Old Testament prophets and the promise of Jesus, who told them He would arise from the grave. I can't imagine watching the events leading to Jesus being put in the tomb. It is easy for us to be critical of the followers of Jesus for scattering, but they saw the events of the crucifixion unfold. Although the last words from Jesus to his disciples were that he would arise on the third day, they lost hope.

I can read the Word of God daily. I know He arose from the grave, but my hope still wanes at times, my faith grows weak, and it seems God doesn't hear my prayers. I may feel it's dark as midnight, but Jesus Christ is risen. He is no longer in the grave. Death gave way to victory. Because He is alive, I too can live. The whole purpose of His Calvary experience was for me to go to heaven and to give me abundant life here on earth. I have hope! No matter what I face, no matter how bad the doctor's report is, and no matter how badly I feel physically, I have hope. As long as there is hope, I can rise from the bed each morning knowing He is with me every step of the way. He cares for me. As His child, I can call on the name of Jesus and the King of Kings is with me.

I can live an abundant life even though I may suffer pain and limitations. It is up to me! He gave me life and life more abundantly, but I must choose to live that abundant life. I've listened to patients in waiting rooms tell total strangers about all their ailments, as if they are trying to prove their situation is more dire than anyone else's. I wish I could lead them through

M.D. Anderson where small babies are taking chemo for cancer. That young child has lost their hair and both the child and parents are going through a difficult situation.

I want to dwell on the good things of God and His blessings in my life! I am blessed beyond measure. I can get out of bed. I can spend time with my sons and their families. To be with my grandchildren is a great joy! I'm blessed to have lived 60 years when I could easily have died at birth, at a very early age when I had my tonsils removed, or at 21 when I had my accident.

God has been good to me. He forgave my sins. He filled me with His spirit and has looked out for me time and time again. I am blessed to watch my sons grow up and now I have five grandchildren. God blessed me with a spouse who loves me and is patient when she could easily walk out on me. She sat in hospital rooms and doctors' offices during difficult times. On many occasions, she sat in the car and cried in the hospital parking garage. She called on friends to join her in prayer and soon she got her strength and faith back to walk back into the hospital room and encourage me. I am truly blessed and that gives me hope!

I know the Word of God is sure. No matter what I may face, I know He will never leave me nor forsake me and will be with me even to the end of the earth. Heaven and earth may pass away but His Word remains forever. His Word is where I turn for comfort and direction when I am discouraged. He is the Captain of my ship and will see me through any storm.

In Acts 3, Peter and John were on their way to prayer when they encountered a lame man begging for alms as they arrived at the temple. I imagine they had seen him in the past, but this time, Peter and John offered him something they had not had before. They recently came from an upper room experience where they received the power of the Holy Ghost. Peter told the lame man they did not have silver and gold, but they had something far more valuable. Peter reached down, took the man's hand, and picked him up. The man received strength in his ankles and could walk. When word spread about the miracle, Peter and

John were taken before Caiaphas, Annas the high priest, and others. Peter and John were asked by what power or name they had performed this miracle. Acts 4:8 tell us Peter, filled with the Holy Ghost, declared this was done by the name of Jesus. They were told they would face sure arrest and possibly death if they continued to preach the name of Jesus. Peter and John met with their group of friends and retold everything that happened and then they prayed. Their prayer is interesting. They did not pray for God to stop the attack or even for God to keep them safe. They prayed for spiritual boldness so they could share their testimony of what God had done in their lives.

My prayer is, "God, give me more than healing. I want boldness to tell of all you've done in my life." God spared my life. He brought my wife and I through some very dark days. We faced times of great struggle and hardship. We've had times when we were unsure how we would make it. Every time,

He took us by the hand, lifted us up and gave us strength when we were weak and broken. I pray God gives us boldness to tell of all His mercy, grace and healing in our lives. I know what the doctors may call chronic pain is only chronic in this life. The old song aptly states: "There is a happy land of promise over in the great beyond, where the saved of earth shall soon the glory share; where the souls of men shall enter and live on forever more, everybody will be happy over there." A day is coming when there will be no chronic pain, no sickness, or brokenness. Our job is to keep the hope of tomorrow until we finish the race.

Chapter 30

BEAUTIFUL, IN HIS TIME

The Bible tells us in Genesis that God created the heaven and the earth. Throughout the Word of God, we are told that He created all things. Ecclesiastes 3:11 **11** *He hath made everything beautiful in his time* (KJV).

The wise man Solomon tells us that not only did God create everything, but in His time, He created everything beautiful. We often find ourselves in ugly situations in our relationships, health, finances, or other areas of life. When we put our situation in the hands of God and submit to Him, He can turn that ugly situation into a beautiful thing that brings glory to God.

I often find myself thinking "what if?" What if I hadn't gone to work for a construction company? What if I hadn't gone up on the building that day? What if...? I can't go back and change anything in the past. I can only move forward. The pain, the suffering, the surgeries, all the scars, and the inadequate feelings must be handed to God. Instead of looking back at what I have missed or focusing on my physical limp and scars, I must focus on the beauty God brought into my life over the years. God made ALL things and HE made ALL THINGS BEAUTIFUL. He makes them beautiful in His timing.

Giving your mess to God and allow Him to work in that situation. He can turn it into something beautiful that will bring Him glory. God can bring a great testimony from any hopeless situation if you are willing to put it totally and completely in His hands.

There are times in my life that things seemed so bleak and dark that nothing beautiful could possibly come out of it, but my testimony of how God had brought me out of that situation helped someone in need. I realized God made that situation beautiful. Relationships that may seem in complete disarray and impossible to reconcile can be restored and made into a beautiful testimony of God's grace and mercy.

If you face health challenges and have been told there is no hope, you can become a great testimony of peace when you give it to Him. Paul wrote some of his greatest letters while sitting under house arrest awaiting his death sentence. Whatever you face, whatever you go through, whatever the situation, and no matter how dark things may seem, by giving it to God, in His time, He will turn it into something beautiful.

I challenge you to place your hope in God and allow Him to work in your life. Allow Him to make what has kept you awake at night into a beautiful overcomer. Revelation 21: **4** *"And God shall wipe away all tears from their eyes; and there shall be no more death, neither sorrow, nor crying, neither shall there be any more pain: for the former things are passed away. 5 And he that sat upon the throne said, Behold, I make all things new. And He said unto me, "Write, for these words are true and faithful."*

I'm living for the day that He takes away all pain and sorrow and wipes away every tear. He will give us a new body with no pain, no scars, no arthritis, or sickness of any kind. Until then, my hope is in Christ Jesus who has endued us with the same power that brought Him out of the grave. We are living for the day when all the struggles of this life are passed, but we still have hope for today. We have a hope that can bring us through any situation or circumstance. We will overcome by the blood of the Lamb and the word of our testimony. He will make my darkest days into something beautiful and give me joy unspeakable.

Chapter 31

2022

In early May 2022, the pain returned to my right leg. It was a little different. Instead of stopping at the right knee, the pain went down to my right foot. There was a burning pain in my leg and it also had that heavy weighted feeling again. I started to stub my toe on the ground as I brought my right foot forward and would stumble or catch myself grabbing onto something nearby to steady myself. The pain in my lower back greatly increased and my headaches became more consistent and far more painful. I had positional headaches which occur when going from lying down to standing up. They occurred mostly in the morning. Later in the day, when I had been up for several hours, the headaches were quite painful and required me to lay down in the bed, with no light and as little noise as possible. My grandchildren are dear to me, and I love hearing them at night when they've had their bath and are playing inside the house with their toys, but the noise was often more than I could take, so I went to the bedroom, turned off the light and would lie down in the bed.

By late May, the pain moved into both legs and got worse by the day. I followed up with Dr. Faraji at Houston Methodist and while there, he ordered a CT-Scan and an MRI, which showed more spinal fluid collecting in the lower back. Dr. Faraji said he was concerned about the amount of spinal fluid I was still losing and wanted me to stay in bed, on my back, as much as possible.

My lower back was very unstable. Dr. Faraji hoped another surgery could be put off for a year, but he now felt there was no choice but to perform surgery as soon as possible.

After returning home to Dripping Springs, my wife took me to an emergency room in Austin, and then a few weeks later to the emergency room at Methodist in Houston where I was admitted to for bone density scans, x-rays, and MRIs. The tests showed the spinal leaks continued and the lower back was in desperate need of surgery. The good news was one of the neurological surgeons who had recently moved could perform the needed surgery in Austin. A few days after returning home from Houston, we saw Dr. Mayer, who said surgery was needed to stabilize my lower back.

While I don't understand the why, I do know God is in control and is working in my life. By praying and asking God to take control of my life, I must put everything in His hands. He is the God who can do all things and His ways are far above mine. In the words of Job 23:10-11 (KJV) *"But He knows the way that I take: when He hath tried me, I shall come forth as gold. 11 My foot held His steps, His way have I kept, and not declined."*

God has been that fourth man in the fire for me time and time again (reference Daniel 3). He will make something beautiful out of this and my testimony will bring glory to God. I would rather not have surgery, but I ask Him to guide my steps and for His will to be done in my life and family. I will align myself with Him. He will not lead me astray. My hope is not in physicians, though I have some great physicians. My hope is in the Great Physician. I know He has an answer for all that I face in the future. John 3:16 tells us simply, "for God so loved." God loves me and will be with me in every situation. I have hope, because I know I am loved by God and His love is never failing.

As we entered the summer of 2022, I still made emergency room visits on a regular basis for pain in my legs and lower back as well as my headaches. One of the doctors at Houston Methodist moved to Austin and set up a state-of-the-art neurological clinic. We felt blessed to see him in Austin instead of driving to Houston for doctor's appointments. We found Dr. Mayer to be a young, caring, patient- oriented neurosurgeon. In June 2022, multiple MRIs showed both my spinal cord and spinal column needed surgery once again. The bones that make up the spinal column were very unstable due to arthritis. The spinal cord still leaked spinal fluid. Surgery to fuse the remaining lumbar discs in my back was scheduled for July 2022. This time, they would need to go through my abdomen instead of my back. After weeks of bedrest, I started another long period of physical therapy. There was little improvement in the heaviness in my legs and I was very prone to falling.

I had a nerve study in October 2022. Dr. Mayer said the nerves going to my legs had been damaged from the spinal cord being mashed flat from large areas of arthritis in the spinal column. The nerves were also damaged from having a very limited amount of spinal fluid reaching them. I thought of the many times a charging cord for my iPhone had gotten bent near the place it plugged into my phone and soon shorted out. The spinal fluid that bathes the nerves had been cut off for such a long time that they could not regenerate. Pamala and I sat in the doctor's office devastated. Dr. Mayer tried to comfort us as we sat in stunned silence with little or no hope offered.

Everything that could be done had been done and now we were given news that left us numb. My wife cried and I sat in disbelief. Dr. Mayer said he had patients who had been given little to no hope of regaining nerve stimulation, and without explanation, regained it 18 months to two years later. He suggested that I walk daily in hopes of stimulating the nerves. We continued physical therapy to help with the stumbling and looked to some experimental procedures to assist with my headaches.

After several bad falls around my house, I decided to put my ego aside and use a cane. Vanity can be difficult to overcome. I don't consider myself to be too vain, but I never wanted to use any device that assisted my walking unless it was needed. On many occasions, I walked without crutches against doctor's orders. I used the crutches for a doctor's appointment, but the doctor always knew that I hadn't followed his orders. This same measure of stubbornness pulled me through some difficult times.

Chapter 32

KEEP WALKING WITH JOY

I resumed my daily walks in November. We had a very early cold front in central Texas. The temperature only reached the mid-30s that week. I was forced to wear four pairs of warm up pants, four sweatshirts, a hoodie, a heavy coat meant more for the ski slopes than central Texas, and my thickest gloves to be reasonably warm. I was determined nothing would stop me from my daily walk. I walked in the cold weather and in the rain. I told my wife I would walk until I broke something or broke through, but I was determined to walk. I walked extremely slow and shuffled my feet more than taking strides, but I walked. Thankfully, the weather improved after the first week, but I realized I still needed gloves to protect my hands when I fell. I took a second hit to my ego by wearing baseball batting gloves each day when I walked. Early on, I fell every few days and took a lot of breaks, but I walked three times a day. Each walk took me about 90 minutes. My shuffling eventually turned into more of a stride. To be honest, I never wanted to show weakness in any way. I felt using a cane, wearing batting gloves, limping, and shuffling were all signs of weakness.

Others thought differently. People stopped me in town and said that I inspired them to walk or do something they had wanted to do for some time. People pulled over in their cars and said my persistence encouraged them. When the pain became severe while walking, I called a family member to pick me up. If no one was available, I found a place to sit until I could go again. Countless people in our neighborhood offered to give me rides home or assist me with whatever I needed. This gave me an open door to tell them my story and let them know God never fails us.

People came to our church after I visited with them on my daily walks. People were drawn to what I considered signs of weakness. What I saw as a weakness had become a strength.

The news about permanent nerve damage in my legs created a low point in our lives. It meant that I would live with heavy and painful legs, stumbling or falling on a daily basis. Almost nightly, I deal with muscle cramps in my legs which are due to all the back issues.

While in prayer, the writings of James came to mind. James, the half-brother of Jesus, who had watched Jesus grow up, and was the pastor of the church in Jerusalem, wrote these words in James 1:2-3 (NKJV) *2 My brethren, count it all joy when you fall into various trials, 3 knowing that the testing of your faith produces 4 But let patience have its perfect work, that you may be perfect and complete, lacking nothing. 5 If any of you lacks wisdom, let him ask of God, who gives to all liberally and without reproach, and it will be given to him. 6 But let him ask in faith, with no doubting, for he who doubts is like a wave of the sea driven and tossed by the wind. 7 For let not that man suppose that he will receive anything from the Lord; 8 he is a double-minded man, unstable in all his ways."*

This doesn't mean I must always be happy. There is a difference between happiness and joy. Several dictionaries say joy is an emotion evoked by wellbeing. James says you can have the joy of the Lord, the strength of the Lord, in the middle of your greatest trials. Happiness depends on our circumstances. Happiness depends on what is going on in my life. It can come and go depending on the environment around me. Happiness is temporary, but I can determine that I will have joy. While I have no control over what I go through, I do have control over how I go through it. I may have questions about why I am going through a trial, but I can have the joy of the Lord in the middle of the trial.

Della, a lady I pastored, served as one of the greatest examples of this. At 75 years old, she was full of life. She began serving the Lord in her late 50s. She was an Austin hippy in the 1960s, used drugs and lived an ungodly life. When she started to serve the Lord, she shared her testimony with prison inmates in Texas. She preached in prison services to some of the worst criminals and saw many receive the baptism of the Holy Spirit. I received a call one evening from her family that Della had been admitted to the hospital. She was in the final stages of cancer and her condition grew dire. Her family asked me to pray for her at the hospital. Della was awake, but she could only speak in a weak voice. She believed God would heal her and she would soon be home. A doctor asked me to share with Della and her family that she was getting placed in hospice and would not live for more than a few days. I spoke to her family first and made sure they understood the seriousness. When I spoke to Della, tears rolled down her face as she whispered that she had a lot to do and she felt God would heal her. The next day, my wife and I went to the hospital to visit Della who had grown very weak and her voice difficult to hear. She waved for us to move our ears down close to her mouth as she whispered, "Everything is going to be okay;

I am headed to Heaven and I am ready." Della didn't want to die, but even in death, she had the joy of the Lord because she knew she was ready to meet the Lord face to face.

There are similarities between my spiritual walk and my daily physical walks. For both, I decide to walk daily, no matter what storms come my way or how I feel physically. I am determined to keep walking daily no matter what is going on in my life. When I go several days without physical or spiritual walking, I quickly digress. If the weather is bad during my physical walks, I drive 30 minutes to the mall and walk there. If we are traveling, I find a place and time to walk. I must be as persistent in my daily spiritual walk as I am in my physical walk or I will pay the price the following day. I know there is a price I will pay for not being consistent.

All of this is true spiritually. I must make up my mind that I will walk with God every day. The Bible is clear that God is looking and searching for people who will serve Him. We are told this in Heb. 11:6: *"But without faith it is impossible to please him: for he that cometh to God must believe that he is, and that he is a rewarder of them that diligently seek him."*

God desires those who seek Him. I MUST make up my mind I will come to Him. To serve God, it takes me making up my mind I will seek Him. I will live for Him in a diligent way. That means I must establish daily spiritual disciplines of prayer, read the word of God, and attend church on a consistent basis. When I attend church, I must do more than be a spectator. I must participate through my worship. If I am not consistent in my daily prayer, reading the word of God, and the other spiritual disciplines needed to serve God, I will pay a price. Each day I do not walk with God, I will pay a price spiritually.

We read in John 4:24, *"God is a Spirit: and they that worship Him must worship Him in spirit and in truth."* The words "spirit" and "truth" are both uncapitalized. This passage doesn't say that we worship God when we feel the Spirit (capital S) but we are to worship with spirit, meaning to worship with passion and enthusiasm. In this passage, Jesus spoke to a Samaritan lady who went to the well for water at a time of day when she likely would not meet other ladies at the well. She experienced relationship issues in her life. I am sure she experienced hurtful relationships as well as hurt from those who talked about her behind her back. After a brief discussion, Jesus says in John 4:13-14 (NKJV*)*

"Jesus answered and said to her, "Whoever drinks of this water will thirst again, **14** *but whoever drinks of the water that I shall give him will never thirst. But the water that I shall give him will become in him a fountain of water springing up into everlasting life."*

Her response was simple, spirited, and passionate. She simply said, "Give me this water that I may not thirst again." She went for water from this well but put that need aside to pursue everything God had for her. She was willing to worship God in spirit (with enthusiasm) as well as in truth (her whole heart). She put aside her embarrassment, hurt, and current needs and asked Jesus for His provision.

I have worshipped while frail in body and weak in voice, but my worship was spirited and with passion because I set aside feeling sorry for myself. I set aside my fear and anxiety and worshipped Jesus Christ for being on the throne and for never failing me. To anyone watching, my worship may not have seemed spirited, but it was with everything I had at that moment. When I worshipped with the passion and enthusiasm I had at that time, I began to feel the joy of the Lord flood over me. That same living water flowed through me afresh and anew.

I watched on many occasions as two different people came to church and sat in the same row. One chose to just observe, and one chose to worship God in spirit and in truth. Without fail, the one who observed left the church blaming the singers, pastor, sound guy, and others for not receiving anything from God.

Those who respond with passion and true worship leave filled with fresh revelation. I cannot survive spiritually being a pew sitter. I must go after what God has for me. I have witnessed many individuals attend church for the first time. They had never really prayed before, but they respond to the preached Word of God. God heals them, sets them free from addictions, or fills them with His spirit all because they worship Him in truth in a passionate, spirited way.

It is interesting that a town full of people showed up to "observe" Jesus as He entered Jericho. Zacchaeus was blessed when Jesus went to his house where they shared a meal and visited one-on-one. Zacchaeus was not a man of the people and was the last person the people would have guessed Jesus would pick to go home with. Zacchaeus did more than just show up. He made the maximum effort to see Jesus. In return, Jesus told him to climb down from the tree. Jesus says, *"it is necessary for me to stay at your house today"* (The Lexham English Bible).

People complained about Jesus going to the home of a sinner, but He always rewards those who try to get to Him.

Mark 10 tells the story of Bartimaeus who sat on the side of the road begging daily. A crowd of people followed Jesus as he passed, leaving Jericho for the last time. Anytime you have a large crowd of people there are many needs, but this blind beggar made the effort to diligently seek Jesus, crying out, *"Jesus, thou son of David have mercy on me."* Jesus responds, *"WHAT wilt thou that I should do unto thee?"* The blind man instantly received his sight.

What would you like for Jesus to do in your life today? I must be diligent in reaching for God. He will always respond to my diligence.

The devil doesn't get concerned about my showing up at church, finding fault with the songs, or criticizing the sermon or worshippers. The devil gets concerned when I attend church with the mindset that I will be diligent in my worship. I will worship in a spirited way, and I will worship Him in truth. We often define that worship as "truth" but the "t" is not capitalized. Truth here does not mean God's truth but it means truly worshipping the Lord with all your heart, soul, and mind. I truly worship Him. I make Him the center of my life. When I truly worship Him, I know He will reward me.

I have determined I will establish daily spiritual disciplines that include praying and reading and studying God's Word. I am always in church if I am possibly able. I am more than a spectator. I respond with spirited worship from a true heart. I will be diligent in worship.

I have been given a report on many occasions by the physicians who had done all they could do for that situation and the moment was bleak. When Pamala and I made up our minds to give God the praise for bringing us to this place in our journey and though we had no idea how to move forward, we were rewarded with the joy of the Lord and the reassurance we were going to make it. There was a peace that goes beyond all understanding that allowed us to lay our heads down at night and sleep without fear or anxiety about what the future held.

Those who say they don't believe in organized religion or don't go to church because of hypocrites at church are missing all that God has for them. There is an old saying that goes something like this "don't drink a cup of poison to spite the one who hurt you." You're drinking spiritual poison if you don't attend church because of someone who may be there.

I've attended quite a few Texas Longhorn football games. There are over 100,000 people in attendance from every background, walk of life, and attitude. There are people there I agree with politically and people in attendance I strongly disagree with politically. There are people at the UT football games I would easily get along with and others that would be difficult for me to find any common ground. Those are things I've never considered as to why I do or do not attend a football game. None of these people will keep me from a football game if I want to go. I 've experienced rude ushers, poor service at concession stands, and bad losses to the opponent. None of these things keep me at home. I attend because I like the Longhorns, some years more than others. Why would I do less for God? Hypocrites need to be at church! Sinners need to be at church! I know there are people who act one way at church and a different way away from church, but those people are everywhere. There is no better place for those people to be than in church where their lives can change. I can't be like the Pharisees who constantly criticized Jesus for healing the sinner or just being with the sinners. Jesus said the sick need the physician, not those who are healthy. The local church is the perfect place for those who are imperfect. I know I am far from perfect. The house of God would be empty on Sundays if only the perfect attended.

I can tell you when I *will* walk tomorrow. It is on my schedule to walk. I look at the weather app on my phone and plan what I will wear when I walk the next day. I know I will experience a lot of pain in my back, my legs, and my feet when I start walking. I will likely battle a headache for much of the walk. I know at the end of my walk I will be shuffling my feet and struggling to make it home. I may need to sit down and rest along the way and sometimes ask someone to pick me up and take me home. If I don't walk, I will be much worse off the following day. Pushing through the pain stimulates and bathes the nerves and muscles in spinal fluid.

The same is true spiritually. I can tell you when I will pray, when I will study my Bible, and that I will be in church for every service possible.

In 2 Kings 13, King Joash went to Elisha, the prophet of God. Elisha was an old man, weak in body, and dying. Joash came to pay his respect to the man of God. Elisha told Joash to open the window and pick up the bow and arrows. He then placed his hands on Joash's hands and told Joash to shoot an arrow out the window. Elisha told Joash that it is symbolic of his victory over

Syria and that he must strike the Syrians until he has destroyed them. Elisha then told Joash to take the arrows and strike the ground. Joash struck the ground three times. 2 Kings 13:19 tells us that the man of God was angry with Joash and said he should have struck the ground five or six times and then he would have struck Syria until he had destroyed the Syrian army. Since he struck the ground only three times, he would only defeat Syria three times. This may seem like a harsh story to us, but the solders in that time would often gather before a battle for something much like a high school pep rally before a football game. The solders took their arrows and beat the ground to build up their spirit and bravado. They beat the ground and boast of how they would destroy their army as they beat the ground with their arrows. They built their enthusiasm as they hit the ground continually with their arrows and spears. This was a way of encouraging themselves and a way to challenge themselves as warriors before they went into battle. They showed one another how enthusiastic they were to go into battle and conquer their enemy. It was that same diligence and spirited display that Elisha looked for in Joash. This is why Elisha was so disturbed when Joash simply tapped the ground three times with the arrows. He showed no enthusiasm and no passion for what God wanted to do in his life.

We know Elisha was promised fourteen miracles, or twice the miracles of Elijah. Elisha was on his death bed and saw only 13 miracles. I wonder if the fourteenth miracle was intended for Joash in his victory over Syria. Instead, it went to an unnamed soldier after Elisha's death. The dead soldier was tossed into a pit and came back to life when his lifeless body touched the bones of Elisha. King Joash missed the miracle of permanently defeating his enemy because he showed no enthusiasm for what God wanted to do.

I believe we can miss what God wants to do in our life by losing enthusiasm for the things of God. It is not always easy to pray, to find time to study, or even to worship in spirit or with passion. When I do not stop and make time for God in my life, I settle for less than what God has for me. When I feel sorry for myself and allow fear and anxiety to overtake me, I begin to settle for a substitute blessing. I allow my adversary to rob me of the blessings and miracles God has for me. When my mind is on my problems and my pains, I settle for a secondary anointing and settle for far less than God has for me in my life. It is easy to worry about the future and worry about things I cannot control. I allow what is rightfully mine to be stolen from me because I have lost my diligence in pursuing what God promised me.

God will sustain and keep me. He will enable me to overcome, but it is up to me to make up my mind each day that I will serve the Lord today. Today, I will worship the Lord in spirit and in truth. I must decide each day. I will keep walking with God until I break through to what He has for me. I will not live with less than God has designed for my life. I will not cower in the corner or allow problems and troubles of this life to cause me to lose my first love and settle for crumbs. God has more for me than I can ever imagine.

In 1 Samuel 30, David suffered a total and utter defeat when he returned to the city of Ziklag and found it burned by the Amalekites. Worse than the damage to the city, was that their wives, their sons, and daughters had been taken captive. The fourth verse tells us that David and his men raised their voices and wept until they had no more strength to weep. These hardened men of war were traumatized and felt hopeless. David not only lost his family, but the people blamed him for this utter defeat and wanted to stone him. David was made a victim of the Amalekite army and a scapegoat for the defeat of Ziklag. He heard his most loyal followers talking about killing him because of their loss. David was attacked on all sides and could have easily thrown in the towel.

There are times we feel devastation. We can allow ourselves to be convinced God no longer hears us. Living for God does not mean we are exempt from the trials of life and times of great agony. When these times come, I cannot make the mistake of believing God made a mistake. John 16:33 says, *"In this world you will have tribulation."* However, what separates the child of God from those in the world is how we respond. In I Samuel 30:6, David is greatly distressed but he responded by "encouraging himself in the Lord" as he "strengthens himself in the Lord." He didn't spend hours wallowing in self-pity and whining to God about everything going wrong in his life. David didn't even spend time talking about how bad he had it, how deep his hurt was, or how greatly he was traumatized.

I have complained to God about my life. It makes me feel better. I'm not saying it is wrong, even David questioned things at times. In Psalm 44:24, he asks, *"Why do you hide your face? Why do you forget our affliction and oppression?"* In Psalm 69:1 (NKJV), David says, *"Save me, O God; for the waters are come in unto my soul. 2 I sink in deep mire, where there is no standing: I am come into deep waters, where the floods overflow me. 3 I am weary of my crying: my throat is dried: mine eyes fail while I wait for my God."*

David told God he was sinking or drowning in utter despair and felt hopeless. If you live long enough, you will find yourself in this place. That is different than "poor me" or "woe- is-me" type thinking. It is okay to tell God your feelings without taking on a mindset of self-pity. Because David didn't feel sorry for himself, he could strengthen himself in the Lord his God. God is not a genie who acts on my command. I believe David strengthened himself in the Lord by remembering the promises of God. He reminds himself of being anointed by Samuel and the times God delivered him when he was willing to **keep walking** and confront his enemy.

I made up my mind to keep walking daily both physically and spiritually. As I walk in the physical and the pain begins to get difficult, I remind myself of God's promises in my life by quoting scripture or singing songs of praise. When I remind myself of God's promises such as Hebrews 13:5 (NKJV)......" *For he hath said, I will never leave thee, nor forsake thee*", I can continue to put one foot in front of the other. The same is true spiritually. When things get difficult and life seems to crash in on me, the best thing to do is to **keep walking**.

I never feel better by dwelling on all my problems. When I make up my mind that I will worship the Lord through His Word, I **keep walking** as I encourage myself with scripture.

"Because thou hast made the Lord, which is my refuge, even the most High, thy habitation; 10 There shall no evil befall thee, neither shall any plague come nigh thy dwelling.11 For he shall give his angels charge over thee, to keep thee in all thy ways. And I put one foot in front of the other and take one more step. I focus on worshipping God in spirit, with passion for all his

blessings and his grace in my life and I continue quoting the promises of God. 12 They shall bear thee up in their hands, lest thou dash thy foot against a stone. 13 Thou shalt tread upon the lion and adder: the young lion and the dragon shalt thou trample under feet." Psalm 91:9 (NKJV)

I **keep walking** spiritually though I'm struggling with relationships or in my health. If I have problems on the job, I keep walking and worshipping the Lord because I know the way to get the joy of the Lord is to worship Him in spirit and in truth.

"And these signs shall follow them that believe; In my name shall they cast out devils; they shall speak with new tongues; 18 They shall take up serpents; and if they drink any deadly thing, it shall not hurt them; they shall lay hands on the sick, and they shall recover." Mark 16:17 (NKJV)

As I quote these promises, each step gets lighter, and my focus goes from my problems to the God of all glory who can bring me through any situation if I just keep walking. There are over 7000 promises of God to us in the Bible for us to strengthen ourselves. After encouraging himself in the Lord and strengthening himself in the Lord, David then asked God, "shall I pursue?" God not only told David to go, but to go and recover all.

One of the greatest truths about being a child of God is that when we are diligent in our worship, when we worship Him in spirit and in truth, God will equip us with the tools we need to fight whatever the enemy throws at us. When David went after the Amalekites, he had 600 men but 200 decided to stay behind. David and 400 men, a much smaller group than the Amalekites,

225

went after what had been stolen. David and his men did not know where the Amalekite army was located. They started in a general direction. David and his men came upon an Egyptian slave who had been part of this Amalekite group that devasted Ziklag. He knew exactly where they were located. He probably took part in the raid of Ziklag himself, fell ill, and his master left him behind. God provided a personal guide for David and his group of 400 men. God always rewards our diligence and consistency.

God provides whatever we need to prevail in the midst of trials as long as we stay diligent to Him and keep a true worshipper mindset. In the end, David and his men not only recovered everything taken from them, but they captured all the herds of livestock of the Amalekites. This was far more than David could have imagined when he returned to Ziklag and found all had been taken and the people talking about killing him and making him pay for their loss. God used this great trial to bless David with so much that He gave from his abundance to those back in Judah. David went from great loss to being greatly enriched not despite his trial, but because of his trial. We may not always profit financially from a trial, but if we are diligent in our worship to God and if we strengthen ourselves in God's Word, we will come out on top. We always profit from our trials.

The things I saw as a sign of weakness when I walked were things I saw as a loss. God used those very things to bring me in contact with people I would have not otherwise contacted.

I do not know what I will face in the future, but I know if I establish a daily lifestyle of worshipping in spirit and in truth, God will bring me out. I must be diligent in keeping God the priority in my life. It is difficult when it seems hell focuses its attacks on your life. Our human reaction is to get in the bed and pull the covers over our head, but I know God will bring me out when I encourage myself in Him. I begin to worship as I remind myself of His promises.

Growing up in the oil fields of east Texas in the home of a pastor, I didn't have a lot. I grew up around kids in my high school who had everything they wanted. Their parents were wealthy from generations of oil money. Their families had houses, jet planes, cars, and everything they desired. I was jealous at times because I saw what I did not have. I wore some of their second-hand clothes. My cousin, Denise, who is more like a sister than a cousin, and I talked often about what we would do if we had the money some of those around us had. Now, many years later, I have stayed in contact with some of those I grew up around. Instead of being jealous, I feel sorry for them. They grew up in homes with things but did not have a relationship with God. I am so thankful for grandparents and parents who knew how to pray and who had a commitment to be in God's house when the doors were open. They established a lifestyle of worship and taught me how to worship despite the trials that we faced. I've watched people who had wealth lose money, fall to addictions, battle relationship issues, and face other struggles that a life without God brings. I have seen others who were once in the church walk away from God and their life was a constant struggle.

Paul and Silas could worship after being beaten, put in prison, and bound (Acts 16). They established an attitude of worshipping God daily. Once in prison, they did what came natural to them. They knew to worship God in spirit and in truth. They had been beaten, they were in bonds, and they were in prison, yet they still worshipped God in such a spirited way that the other prisoners took notice. At midnight, or at a time that things seemed the bleakest, they broke out in a worship service. Acts 16:25 makes it clear they do more than give mental assent to God. Verse

25 clearly says *"... the prisoners heard them."* Verse

26 starts with, *"And suddenly there was a great earthquake so that the foundations of the prison were shaken and immediately all the doors were opened and every one's bands were loosed."* Not only were Paul and Silas delivered through their worship, but the doors of the prison opened. The jailer was about to kill himself when Paul said, "we are all here, don't kill yourself." The jailer cleaned their wounds and took care of their needs, and then asked how he could experience what Paul and Silas had working in their life. He and others were baptized. These were saved all because Paul and Silas worshipped God in spirit and in truth in prison. Had Paul and Silas waited until they were placed in prison before establishing a habit of worship, it would have been difficult for them to turn to praise at midnight. Worship came naturally to them at this most difficult time.

It was a hit to my ego to walk daily through my neighborhood while limping and shuffling as well as walking with a cane and wearing batting gloves, but establishing a daily walk was one of the few things outside of the miraculous that would help the nerves in my legs. I made up my mind to do it. Soon I had people telling me they had taken note of my consistency and were moved to either exercise or do other activities they had wanted to do but had put off for various reasons.

My daily walk with God will help others around me. People will take note of my spiritual consistency. Matthew 9 tells of a lady with the issue of blood touching the hem of Jesus' garment and receiving her healing. Five chapters later, many others sought to touch the hem of His garment, and as many as touched were made perfectly whole. People take note of your sacrifice and your consistent life of worship.

I made up my mind to keep walking. I put one foot in front of the other each day. I keep walking physically and spiritually. Some days are more difficult than others and the walk is not easy. If I stop today, tomorrow will be more difficult, so I will keep walking. Paul said, "I press toward the mark." Some days I must press to continue walking, but I will walk. My focus is not always on the future but simply the next step.

I will continue pressing and pushing to maintain my walk with God. I will worship Him no matter what. The only way to get the joy I need is to **keep walking**. If I keep walking, I can recover everything the enemy has stolen from me, and I will recover my joy, peace of mind, family, and relationships. The winds blow and the hills seem steep at times, but I **keep walking**. He has never failed me yet. He has kept every promise, so I **keep walking**. Each step takes me closer to the promises God has for my life.

I will always worship him. I will **keep walking**. I will not base my walk on my feelings, but on God's promises and the joy that comes from knowing Him. Each day I will walk with Him and He will walk with me. I will **keep walking** with God because there is no place to stop. My only hope lies in Jesus Christ and my relationship with Him. I am thankful I have a relationship with the Lord. I know I cannot stand without Him.

I do not know what I face in the future, but I can face it if I continue my walk with God. When I look back on what God has brought me through, I see He gave me a testimony.

His eye is on the sparrow, and I know He watches over me.